P9-DNB-788

GRASS-FED NATION

Praise for Graham Harvey's previous books

The Killing of the Countryside

'He explodes the myth of cheap food with a few simple statistics'

John Humphrys, *New Statesman*

'I fully support this book's profound and Blake-like charge'

John Fowles, *Sunday Times*

'A modern *Grapes of Wrath*'

Simon Jenkins, *The Times*

'A brave, much-needed book'

John Vidal, *The Guardian*

'A forceful, informed and authoritative account of the state of farming and the countryside'

Bryn Green, *Spectator*

We Want Real Food

'Passionate, well-argued and thought-provoking'

Independent on Sunday

'Explains clearly that we can all make a change in what we eat and radically improve our health'

The Ecologist

'A book that deserves to be properly chewed over'

Felicity Lawrence, *The Guardian*

GRAHAM HARVEY

GRASS-FED NATION

GETTING BACK THE FOOD WE DESERVE

ICON

Published in the UK in 2016
by Icon Books Ltd, Omnibus Business Centre,
39–41 North Road, London N7 9DP
email: info@iconbooks.com
www.iconbooks.com

Sold in the UK, Europe and Asia
by Faber & Faber Ltd, Bloomsbury House,
74–77 Great Russell Street,
London WC1B 3DA or their agents

Distributed in the UK, Europe and Asia
by Grantham Book Services,
Trent Road, Grantham NG31 7XQ

Distributed in the USA
by Publishers Group West,
1700 Fourth Street, Berkeley, CA 94710

Distributed in Canada
by Publishers Group Canada,
76 Stafford Street, Unit 300, Toronto, Ontario M6J 2S1

Distributed in Australia and New Zealand
by Allen & Unwin Pty Ltd,
PO Box 8500, 83 Alexander Street,
Crows Nest, NSW 2065

Distributed in South Africa
by Jonathan Ball, Office B4, The District,
41 Sir Lowry Road, Woodstock 7925

Distributed in India by Penguin Books India,
7th Floor, Infinity Tower – C, DLF Cyber City,
Gurgaon 122002, Haryana

ISBN: 978-1-78578-076-9

Typeset in Minion by Marie Doherty

Printed and bound in the UK by Clays Ltd, St Ives plc

Contents

ABOUT THE AUTHOR

Graham Harvey has written on food and farming for *Farmers Weekly*, the *Sunday Times*, the *Daily Mail*, *New Scientist* and *Country Life*. For three years he wrote the 'Old Muckspreader' column in *Private Eye*. In the mid-1980s he joined the script-writing team of *The Archers*, since when he has written more than 600 episodes of the BBC drama; he is currently the programme's agricultural advisor. Graham's first book, *The Killing of the Countryside*, was winner of the BP Natural World Book Prize. He is also co-founder of the country's leading conference on low-input, ecological agriculture – the Oxford Real Farming Conference.

To the memory of Walter Yellowlees
A Doctor in the Wilderness

Introduction (Paradise Wasted)

If you needed a way to assess the general state of modern Britain you probably wouldn't choose to count its hedgehogs. You might take look at the FTSE share index, I suppose. Or perhaps the current level of spending on the health service. But the number of hedgehogs? Unlikely, I'd say.

Not so long ago these oddly endearing animals were the butt of many a stand-up comic's jokes. In the face of danger they're in the habit of rolling their spiny bodies into a tight ball, a defence mechanism that's spectacularly unsuccessful against trucks. Which meant you often used to see them dead on the roads.

These days you rarely see a squashed hedgehog. This doesn't mean we're driving any better. It simply means there aren't nearly so many around as there used to be. Some surveys show their numbers may have halved in a decade.[1] But it's not the traffic that's killing them. It's the countryside.

The hedgehog is just one of a long list of wild species that have fallen victim to what's happening in rural Britain. Not long ago our countryside provided a home for huge numbers of wild animals, birds and plants. Today it has become a hostile place for many of them. This ought to come as a wake-up call because it's rapidly becoming a hostile place for us as well.

Even though most of us live in towns and cities we retain a deep affection for, not to mention pride in, our countryside. We tune in to wildlife and countryside programmes in our droves. In the annual orgy of national flag-waving that is the Last Night of the Proms, we sing passionately about bringing Jerusalem to our 'green and pleasant land'. But while it may still be green, much of it isn't that pleasant any more.

It's been taken over by what could almost be described as an alien culture. It furthers the interests of a few, while rapidly ruining things for the rest of us. Our elected politicians seem unwilling to step in. In fact most of them welcome the changes as 'progress'. The media, meanwhile, rarely subject this rural occupation to any degree of rigorous examination.

This book is about the Britain we all seem to have turned our backs on – the 70 or so per cent of our land that our food comes from. It's the part of our environment that we engage with most deeply through the purchasing decisions we make at the checkout, and that also has the biggest effect on our own health. If wild species are being destroyed it's we who are doing it. And in our failure to consider the consequences of those decisions, we're almost certainly harming ourselves too. The two problems are deeply interlinked.

Managed in all our interests, the countryside could help solve many of the nation's greatest challenges, from public health to climate change. Instead it's making all our problems a great deal worse.

For people of my generation growing up in the years following World War Two, good food was generally affordable by everyone. Imports were higher then, but food produced at home was from a countryside rich in wildlife. No one saw biodiversity as the enemy of productivity. They were simply the two sides of a sustainable food system.

Today that system has been largely demolished. In its place we have poorer food laden with toxic residues. Our wildlife is vanishing. And where once we had a secure food supply, our ability to feed ourselves in the future looks ever more uncertain.

What it adds up to is the theft of our food heritage. Much of our farmland no longer produces the foods evolution prepared us for. The consequences for the nation are potentially more serious even than the damage caused by the banking crisis. It's happened as a result of poor science and corporate ruthlessness. But mostly because of our own lack of interest.

In the old days of coal-mining, the miner's caged canary provided an early warning that the build-up of toxic gases had reached dangerous levels. In the fields of modern Britain it's bird populations that have taken some of the biggest hits from modern farming methods.

Among the endangered species is the turtle dove, whose gentle purr was once evocative of summer. In Chaucer's time it was known as the bird of love. Its most important food plant is a delicate, smoky-leaved wildflower known as fumitory, a plant that used to be common in arable fields. In today's fields the plant has all but disappeared. It seems the turtle dove may soon follow.

Maybe we should make this bird our new canary? Let

its decline be a warning that we're in grave danger from an enemy within. A revival in the bird's numbers will signal an improvement in the health and well-being of all of us. This book is about a national – and international – tragedy and how, if we all get stuck in, we can fix it.

CHAPTER 1

Darwin's diet

It's late autumn and the river running through my local town has turned the colour of a cappuccino. This doesn't come as any great surprise. It's happening with monotonous regularity these days. Most of the time the river runs a sort of dark, grey-green colour. But get a few hours of rain and it's reborn as a coffee-coloured torrent.

Around the same time there's a report in the media about the diabetes epidemic currently sweeping through Britain. According to one online medical journal, the number of people with 'pre-diabetes' – many of whom will go on to develop the full-blown disease – has tripled in eight years. Apparently one in three of us are now affected.[1]

There's also a lot in the news about cancer. The number of new diagnoses has gone up by nearly 40 per cent over the past couple of decades. According to researchers, half of us will develop the disease at some point in our lives.[2]

These may seem like random events – the coffee-coloured river and the rising tide of disease in Britain. But to an old farming journo like me there's a clear link. What happens to our rivers – and more precisely, what happens to the land they flow through – is connected with the level of disease in society. Unfortunately the experts who deal in public health don't get to talk to the ones who worry about polluted waterways, so no one's joined up the dots. If they did they'd realise that, just as there's a common cause, there's a remedy out there, too.

Over the years I've spent a fair bit of time checking out the colour of our local river. Even though the changes are happening a lot more often than they used to, it still comes as a shock to see the brown stain. I imagine this is how the River Euphrates looked when the Fertile Crescent – cradle of agriculture and western civilisation – was turning into desert. Or the River Tiber in Rome. The citizens must have been watching this colour switching at around the time the empire was falling apart. But who would believe it could happen in modern, enlightened, scientifically-literate Britain?

Though it's scarcely believable, we humans are fast destroying our most precious natural resource: the soil that feeds us. Across the world we get 99 per cent of our food from the land. Yet each year we allow 10 million hectares of farmland to be destroyed by soil erosion.[3]

According to the World Health Organization, two-thirds of the people on our planet are malnourished, which means either they're not getting the nutrients they need or their dietary nutrients are unbalanced.[4] Despite this, soil is being lost from farmland up to 40 times faster than it can be formed by natural processes. While it's true that erosion rates are highest in Asia, Africa and South America, British and American farmers are still destroying soils far faster than they can be replaced by natural processes.[5]

Long before soils collapse they become dysfunctional. Their ability to supply nutrients to crop plants is impaired.

This is why the milky-brown waters are a warning we ignore at our peril. Roughly interpreted they mean there's going to be more sickness around; more of what health experts call 'non-communicable' diseases. Weird though it may seem, the stained waters tumbling under a Somerset river bridge are a fair indication that things are going to get a whole lot worse.

Whenever we hear of someone being struck down with cancer or heart disease, most of us think of it as bad luck and nothing more. We try to cut down the risks by giving up smoking or eating more sensibly or reducing our alcohol intake. Apart from that we hope for the best and get on with our lives. Doctors reassure us that we're all living longer. Diseases like cancer in our later years are the price we have to pay.

However, this isn't what they used to think. A century ago there was a broad medical consensus that the 'diseases of civilisation', as they were called, were caused by processed foods, particularly those rich in sugar and refined white flour. The evidence came mostly from doctors who'd had experience working overseas.[6]

Wherever the Europeans settled they took their western foods with them – white bread, cakes, biscuits and sugar. Where local people steered clear of the stuff and stuck with their traditional diets, diseases like cancer and heart disease were rarely seen. But when the locals took to western foods, the new diseases started to appear. They included obesity, diabetes, heart disease, cancer, tooth decay, gallstones, varicose veins and many more.[7]

Typical were reports coming out of Africa and published in the medical journals of the early 20th century. Doctors started seeing the first cancer cases in places where the local people mixed with Europeans and copied their diets. But they rarely saw the disease in people who had stayed true to their ancestral diets. Reports from doctors working with native Americans told a similar story. Cancer cases were rare or non-existent in most tribes. Among Inuit peoples, whose diets were made up mainly of seal meat, high in saturated fat, cancer cases were hardly ever seen. Nor was heart disease.

The consensus that modern diseases were the result of eating refined carbohydrates lasted until the early 1970s. It was then discounted because it didn't fit easily with the new theory that saturated fat was a major risk factor. Today that fat–disease connection has been largely discredited. Researchers now say the earlier health advice that we should reduce saturated fat in the diet was never supported by the evidence. There was no chance that it would reduce heart disease rates.[8]

Yet across the western world dieticians and the manufacturers of low-fat foods continue to spread the fable that saturated fat is bad. And the medical world has so far failed to reinstate and investigate the old theory linking modern disease to processed foods.

In the absence of a clear lead from the medical world, evolutionary biologists have stepped into the healthy diet debate. Like doctors of the early 20th century they're convinced it's sugar and starchy grains such as wheat and rice that are to blame for the dire state of our health. And we have agriculture to thank for it!

Jared Diamond, author of *Guns, Germs and Steel*, described farming as the worst-ever mistake made in human history.[9] We choose to think of the human story as one of unbroken progress from primitive tribal societies to our modern world. We view the switch from hunter-gathering to farming as a crucial step along the way. Who wouldn't swap the hard work and insecurity of hunting and foraging for the ease and plenty of farming communities?

But in reality, says Diamond, this momentous change didn't make life any better. Instead it made things a good deal worse. As hunter-gatherers we had enjoyed diets rich in protein and well-balanced for other nutrients. But as farmers we started eating starchy foods, particularly cereal crops like wheat. We probably didn't have much choice in the matter. There were too many mouths to feed. But in making the switch to agriculture we gave up a healthy diet for a far poorer one.

Hunter-gatherers ate almost everything that was edible in the natural world around them. This meant they enjoyed a very diverse diet, which included dozens of plant species in season. By contrast, farmers concentrate on growing a few staple crops with high yields.

Today we rely on wheat, rice and potatoes for a large part of our energy intake. In other parts of the world, farmers have relied on grains such as millet, barley and rye as food staples, along with starchy crops like cassava and taro. While these are rich in calories and can be grown in large quantities, they often contain far fewer vitamins and minerals than the wild plants harvested by hunter-gatherers.[10]

Archaeological evidence shows that in the period when

human beings were changing from hunting to farming – around 12,000 years ago – there was a rapid decline in their bone density. Their skeletons became more fragile and subject to fractures, a weakness that continues to this day.[11] At the same time the average height of human beings fell, and there was a big increase in infectious disease, iron-deficiency anaemia and degenerative conditions of the spine.

Studies on human stature over the past 40,000 years show that in Europe humans became shorter at the end of the Ice Age, partly because they adapted to warmer climates. As agriculture took hold their stature declined even further. It was only in the mid-20th century that Europeans returned to the height of their caveman ancestors.[12]

The starchy, high-carbohydrate diets of the first farmers kept more people alive. But they reduced the quality of life because of the illnesses they caused. Ten thousand years later nothing much has changed. Drive around the countryside today and you'll see field after field of those same starchy crops – potatoes, barley, sugar beet, and most of all wheat. They're destined to be processed into the very foods that doctors a century ago identified as bad for our health.

To make matters worse, the crops that are killing us are also killing the soils on which we all depend for our food and our health. The chemicals used to grow these crops are steadily destroying the life of the soil. To stay healthy and productive, soils rely on a vast underground army of living organisms from microscopic bacteria to earthworms.

But the high-yielding wheats and oilseed crops that fill our fields can't survive without a routine fix of chemical fertilisers and pesticides. Unfortunately these same chemicals damage the living communities of the soil. Robbed of this living component, soils are less able to supply nutrients to plants.

To compensate, farmers have to apply even more agrochemicals, which further damages soil organisms. The whole soil ecosystem is caught up in a vicious spiral to destruction. It ends when the weakened soil becomes so unstable it's easily eroded away by water and wind.

This is why so many of the world's rivers are changing colour. They're stained with the remnants of dying soils being washed away to the sea. It's why we ought to take notice. The stains are a sure sign, not only that we're growing the wrong foods, but that we're demolishing the only guarantee we have of a healthy future – fertile soil. Offhand I can't think of a more effective way for a civilisation to destroy itself, apart, perhaps, from engaging in nuclear war.

As it happens my local river – the Tone – rises quite close to where I live in west Somerset. So I get to see the whole colour-change process. Whenever we get a spell of heavy rain, torrents of red-brown floodwater come gushing off the fields and down the steep lanes. They swell the river and stain it orange-brown as it flows under the town centre bridge in Taunton. Much of this cargo of silt will be dumped in the Somerset Levels, where the river takes a slow, meandering course to join the River Parrett.

The river runs orange-brown because that's the colour of our local soils, and because those soils are now sick. Healthy soils don't get washed away in rainstorms. Soils capable of growing strong, nutrient-rich crops don't go floating off downstream. They don't clog up ditches and drains, or deposit a sandpit at the side of the road. They stay put. The run-off water – if there is any – is clear.

That's how it is in our towns and cities most of the time. When I drive through my local town, even during a heavy rainstorm, the rain that comes gushing down the street isn't a muddy-brown. It's always clear. Our parks and suburban gardens keep soil in good shape. It's the countryside where the damage is at its worst.

Shockingly, it's modern farming methods that pose the main threat to our food supply. And all to produce crops that will make many of us sick.

In his book *The Story of the Human Body*, evolutionary biologist Daniel Lieberman coins the phrase 'mismatch diseases' for the sort of illnesses that afflict us today.[13] He defines them as diseases that result from our Paleolithic bodies being poorly adapted to our modern environment and way of life.

For example, natural selection over several million years adapted the human body for a diverse diet of fruit, tubers, wild game, seeds, nuts, and other foods that are rich in fibre but low in sugar. So it's hardly surprising that we develop illnesses such as type 2 diabetes and heart disease from consistently eating foods that are loaded with sugar and depleted of fibre.

Lieberman produces a list of nearly 50 non-infectious illnesses that he suggests could be evolutionary mismatches. They include coronary heart disease, type 2 diabetes, depression, some cancers, Alzheimer's, Crohn's disease, glaucoma, hypertension, myopia, metabolic syndrome, multiple sclerosis and osteoporosis.

It's an alarming catalogue of modern ailments, and Lieberman stresses that in the absence of good data it's only a hypothesis, a guess. Even so, he believes it's not possible to over-emphasise the importance of mismatch diseases. We're most likely to die from a mismatch disease. We're most likely to suffer from disabilities caused by mismatch diseases. Mismatch diseases account for the bulk of healthcare spending throughout the world.

Why, then, are our fields full of crops that will be turned into the starchy, sugary foods that will probably see us off? Our countryside is quite capable of producing the kinds of foods we once enjoyed as hunter-gatherers. We don't have to head out to the woods with our bows and arrows. As a society we're smart enough to reorganise our agriculture so that it produces the kinds of foods that protect our health rather than the deadly stuff it's now turning out. As we'll discover, there's one simple dietary change we could all make to put ourselves and our countryside back on the path to good health.

The reason why our soils seldom used to disappear downriver was that farmers always planted at least some of their fields with one particular life-enhancing crop. It's so familiar that few of us even think of it as a crop at all. It's grass – or rather, pasture, because it usually included plants such as clovers and herbs as well as grasses.

Over the centuries, farmers learned that they couldn't go on growing food crops year after year on the same land or it would quickly become exhausted. For a long time the only remedy was to rest the land, to leave it lying fallow. Later they discovered that rather than leave the land lying idle it was more profitable to sow it to pasture and graze it with cattle or sheep. In some mysterious way this would revitalise the land, giving it a new burst of fertility so it would grow more food crops.

What these farmers had stumbled upon was the power of crop rotations. Here was the secret of a dependable food supply. Somewhere around the middle of the 18th century the mixed farm was born. It was to create a revolution as momentous as the industrial revolution that would follow.

By alternating grassland and grazing with the growing of food crops such as wheat, farmers succeeded in harnessing nature's methods for keeping land fertile. No chemical fertilisers were required. No pesticides. The whole system was driven by the power of the sun, channelled through pasture plants and the microscopic organisms of the soil.

The mixed farm turned Britain into a premier-division farming nation. It fed a growing population at a time when our industrial towns were rapidly expanding. And the foods it produced – grass-fed meat; grass-fed milk, butter and cheese; pasture-raised poultry and eggs – were near-perfect foods for human nutrition.

By including pasture into their crop rotations these pioneering farmers had, in effect, recreated the foods of hunter-gatherers. The Paleolithic diet – the diet of hunter-gatherers – was rich in the meat of animals grazing on wild, natural grassland. The new cropping pattern of the mixed farm included species-rich grasslands not so very different from the wild grasslands of the forest glade and the savannah. The meat this produced was scarcely any different from that eaten by our early ancestors.

Today scientists have begun to discover the health-enhancing benefits of foods from pasture-fed animals. In the popular media, debates over the health value of fresh foods all too often end up in a sterile argument over the pros and cons of organic produce. But we ignore the change that would bring about a huge improvement in our nutrient intakes: the reintroduction of grass-fed foods into our daily diets.

As well as improving our health, pasture and grazing would make our farming more sustainable and our food supply more secure. Science is at last beginning to reveal the way pasture enriches the land and stops soil eroding away downriver. Ironically this is the very time when many farmers are deciding they no longer need pasture to keep their land in good shape. Most now believe they can do the same job using chemical fertilisers and pesticides.

The muddy rivers are a sure sign that they've got it wrong. And we're all paying a high price in degenerative disease. Jared Diamond's savage condemnation of agriculture turns out to be true. But it doesn't have to be. Farms – not the health service or drug companies – are our best hope of leading long and healthy lives. We simply have to make sure our food comes from the right sort of farm.

In the 2.5 million or so years before agriculture came along, we humans went around eating the foods that nature provided. We hunted grazing animals and harvested plants, berries and nuts from the well-stocked forests. Birds' eggs in season were an occasional treat.

Tribes living close to the seashore or a lakeside acquired a taste for fish and shellfish. Some scientists think it was this habit of fish-eating that led to the rapid increase in the size of the human brain.

On these natural foods human beings stayed in tip-top physical condition. This is not to say life was a bed of roses. Far from it. It could be brutish and short. Chasing after woolly mammoths or wild cattle was fraught with danger. But if you could avoid getting injured, the chances were you'd be able to keep up the chase without becoming exhausted. You'd easily manage the stone-age equivalent of two dozen flights of stairs without becoming breathless or showing any great increase in heart rate.

In hunter-gatherer communities even ordinary members of the tribe had the stamina and fitness we'd associate with top athletes today. This was partly because of their physical activity but also because they were generally well nourished. Unless there had been some local environmental catastrophe, people were able to provide their bodies with exactly the right nutrients to keep them functioning at peak efficiency. We were part of nature's grand plan. We ate the foods that evolution had prepared us for. We hadn't yet become smart enough – or crazy enough – to make our own.

In those pre-farming times human diets were rich in

protein and essential fatty acids, especially linoleic acid (an omega-6 fatty acid) and alpha-linolenic acid (an omega-3 fatty acid). They were high in saturated fats, the sort that until recently were supposed to be bad for us. What didn't figure much in our diets were sweet things. Ripe fruits and berries were highly seasonal, and honey would also have been a periodic delicacy. There were no cereal grains. Most carbohydrates came from vegetables and were of the complex, slowly-digested form. And there were, of course, no processed foods.

We humans obtained all the nutrients we needed to thrive and spread across the planet. We flourished, not simply because we ate the foods that evolution had adapted us for, but also because those foods were themselves rich in nutrients. The animals we hunted on the plains and grasslands had grazed and browsed on the vegetation they themselves needed to stay healthy. And those grasses, shrubs and trees had grown in fertile soils, enriched by flourishing populations of microbes.

You could even say the teeming masses of microscopic life below the soil surface were themselves perfectly nourished. They were fed by the wild profusion of plants that handed them 'sweeteners' or exudates, sugary compounds passed through their roots. Powered by the energy of the sun, the vast, interconnected web of life on Earth did the job of distributing and recycling nutrients. Each organism had its place, and each received the nutrients it needed. Like other species on Earth, humans merged seamlessly into a well-functioning ecosystem.

That was until we humans hit on the idea of growing our own food. We started cultivating grasses with large seed-heads, the beginning of cereal growing. We also learned how to domesticate food animals such as cattle and pigs, herding them across the open lands we had cleared of trees. Farming was born. Since then the quality of human nutrition has headed steadily downhill.

In modern western agriculture, crop growing is now the main activity. Drive around much of Britain today and you'll see fields full of the same few plants – wheat, sugar beet and yellow-flowering oilseed rape. And the most important of these is wheat. We now grow massive amounts of the stuff, far more than we can ever eat. We get rid of the surplus by feeding half of it to animals, mostly pigs and poultry, but also to dairy cows and beef cattle, animals for which cereal grains, in any quantity, are neither natural nor healthy.

As a result our diets are unbalanced – depleted of some essential nutrients and over-rich in substances we could well do with less of. Add to this our taste for highly processed products – cakes, biscuits, white bread and the rest – and you have a recipe for disaster. Our bodies are loaded up with materials they weren't designed to handle.

A growing number of nutrition experts now recommend that we give up the foods that followed the farming revolution and stick to the kinds of foods chosen by our hunter-gatherer ancestors. Doctor and nutritionist Andrew Stringer – author of *The Food Fallacy* – recommends our 'ancestral diet' as the best way to stay free of chronic, degenerative disease. The diet includes meat from grazing animals; fish including shellfish;

green, leafy vegetables; seasonal fruits, berries and nuts; and occasional eggs.[14]

Loren Cordain, a leading researcher in environmental medicine, put together the essential nutritional principles as part of his Paleo diet, sometimes known as 'the caveman diet'. To stay fit he recommends that we eat a relatively large amount of animal protein and far fewer carbohydrates than most modern diets recommend.[15] And these carbohydrates should come – not from sugar or starchy foods like grain and potatoes – but from fruits and vegetables. Cordain also recommends that we eat 'moderate' amounts of fat. These should be what he describes as 'good' fats of the kinds known as 'monounsaturated' and 'polyunsaturated' fats.

This new hunter-gatherer style of eating emphasises the importance of meat from grazing animals. Yet modern agriculture, with its obsession for growing wheat, is fast removing them from large stretches of the British landscape.

Not long ago I took a long, slow drive through the East Anglian countryside. I was on a cattle hunt. It was early June and the trees were draped in spring foliage. The hedgebanks were crowded with wildflowers. This was just the time you'd expect to see cattle grazing on lush, green pastures.

I left the motorway at Stevenage and took minor roads through the rural heartlands of Hertfordshire and Essex. On my journey I passed through villages that might have come straight from P.G. Wodehouse – Buntingford, Starling's Green, Steeple Bumpstead. The fields were dark green with young wheat crops or yellow with the flowers of oilseed rape. But there were no cattle to be seen. This came as something of a shock. A few decades earlier you'd have seen plenty of them, even in a part of Britain not traditionally known as 'livestock country'.

As an agricultural student I'd made a similar journey back in the 1960s. In those days there were plenty of mixed farms – farms with pasture and grazing in the rotation as well as crops. Grazing animals were a familiar sight. Today they have all but vanished from many parts of eastern Britain.

I pressed on with my search along quiet country roads. By the time I reached Sudbury I'd clocked up more than 50 miles. And not a single grazing animal had I seen. At that point I called it a day and headed home.

The reason animals have disappeared from the fields is that farmers find it more profitable to keep them in sheds. They can then plough their pasture fields, freeing up the land for growing crops. The traditional landscape of mixed farming, with its patchwork of grazing fields and crop fields, has been turned into a wide-open arable prairie. This change has happened because people in western countries like Britain have invented a whole new way of eating.

We've turned our backs on the foods nature provided. Instead we've been persuaded to eat a range of processed, food-like products. Pies and pastries, pasta and pizzas; cooking oils and yellow-fat spreads; white bread and biscuits. To man and woman the hunter-gatherer all these would have been unrecognisable. But not to man and woman the Tesco-shopper or the Lidl-browser. In my own favourite coffee shop it's virtually impossible to find anything to eat that isn't made with refined white flour.

Our chief public-service broadcaster has even developed a hit TV show, *The Great British Bake Off*, celebrating the commodities that now pour off our farms – wheat, vegetable oil and sugar. We've made a festival of the very things that are making many of us ill.

At the same time we've transformed what were once healthy, nutrient-rich foods like beef, milk and dairy foods into far less healthy products. We've done it by taking cattle off the species-rich pasture that evolution prepared them for. Instead we keep them shut up in barns where we feed them on high-energy foods such as cereal grains and high-protein foods like soya.

It's often said 'we are what we eat'. But when it comes to meat it would be truer to say 'we are what our animals eat'. And what our animals are eating in ever greater amounts are the same starchy foods that are damaging us. We're all busily degrading every part of our diet.

For thousands of years the countryside provided us with foods rich in nutrients, the foods that kept us healthy. Today the crops that fill our countryside aren't so much foods as industrial raw materials. They're grown for manufacturing companies to process into edible products that scarcely merit the name 'food'. Or they're grown as animal feed for factory farms to turn into second-rate versions of the foods that once sustained us. It's hard to believe that we could have devised such a crazy food system.

In her book *The Obesity Epidemic* nutritionist Zoe Harcombe analyses the government's Family Food Survey to find out the sort of things we're all eating these days.[16] The government figures split our foods into 24 categories from fish to biscuits. The stuff we eat most of comes under the heading 'other cereal products'. Accounting for over 10 per cent of our daily calorie intake, it includes breakfast cereals, pasta, pizza, rice pudding, frozen cakes and pastries, cake and pudding mixes.

The next most popular category is 'bread'. Then in third place come 'other meat and meat products'. Of these, three-quarters are processed meats combined with yet more starchy foods – pies, pasties, sausage rolls and puddings. Zoe calculates that one-third of our average calorie consumption comes from these three food categories.

It seems we get no less than 1,536 calories a day from processed foods, with just 491 calories coming from 'real foods', such things as meat and fish, milk, cheese, eggs, real dairy products, fresh fruit and vegetables, real fats such as butter and olive oil, and whole grains.

It's clear now why the countryside has changed. The farmed landscape, once designed around the growing of real, nourishing food, has been reshaped for the production of processed products. Vast areas of our best farmland are now dedicated to growing low-cost cereals, rapeseed oil and sugar. Even the real foods – meat, milk, cheese and eggs – have been downgraded by the need to find a use for the torrent of industrial starches and vegetable oils pouring from our arable fields.

We've given up our ancestral foods for manufactured fakes. This is the principal reason so many of us are succumbing to modern diseases such as heart disease, cancer, diabetes and the rest of them. Our hunter-gatherer ancestors didn't get them. As long as they avoided accidents, infections, violence and predators, they stayed healthy, lean and strong throughout their long lives.[17]

We weren't made to go down with these conditions either, at least not on anything like the present scale. But while we choose to let manufacturing companies feed us rather than nature, the epidemic can be guaranteed to continue.

Here's the reason healthcare costs are swallowing up more and more of our national wealth. Here's why Britain's National Health Service can barely keep up with demand. Yet in an odd way it's good news. It means we have a solution. We could return to our heritage foods, the foods our ancestors thrived on. Our ancestral diet.

Long before there was any kind of health service – long before ordinary people could afford to see a doctor – food was our medicine. And food was the traditionally-grown plants and traditionally-raised animals from a fertile countryside. Everyone knew this. Each generation learned what was good to eat from the people who'd gone before.

Today we look to experts to tell us the things we should be eating. Instead of our parents and grandparents we rely on dieticians, nutritionists and, sometimes, research scientists. We expect them to unravel the mind-numbingly complex interactions between our bodies and the materials we put into them. It's not surprising they sometimes get it wrong. And when they finally arrive at the right answer it's often long after real damage has been done.

Fortunately the laws of nature don't change. The foods that made us healthy 10,000 years ago are the very same foods that would make us healthy today. They are what they always have been – the traditionally-grown and unprocessed foods from a fertile, diverse, brimming-with-life countryside. And at the very heart of this power-house system are grazing animals.

One of the most remarkable studies on the link between food and health was carried out by an American dentist, now hardly remembered. In the early years of the 20th century Weston A. Price ran a flourishing dental practice in the industrial city of Cleveland, Ohio. At the time, people in his home city were abandoning their traditional diets in favour of the new, manufactured foods – white bread, margarine, pasteurised milk and refined white sugar. He saw the results daily in his surgery. Most of his adult patients had rampant tooth decay, often accompanied by degenerative diseases such as arthritis, osteoporosis, diabetes and chronic fatigue.

In the early 1930s Price gave up his dental practice. He and his wife set out on a series of epic journeys to some of the most remote places on the planet. His plan was to visit peoples untouched by 'civilisation' – peoples reputed to display remarkable health, and to enjoy long lives, untroubled by sickness and disease. He wanted to find out whether these stories were true. And if they were, he wanted to know what foods these peoples ate.

The couple's first visit was to a valley high in the Swiss Alps. Until the building of an eleven-mile railway tunnel a few years earlier, the Loetschental Valley in the Bernese Oberland had been virtually isolated from the outside world.

There Price was astonished to find children tough enough to walk barefoot in freezing mountain streams without ill effects.

They seldom caught colds, and infections were virtually unknown. No case of tuberculosis had ever been seen in the valley community, though the people had been exposed to the bacillus. The children's teeth and gums were in perfect condition, Price discovered, with no sign of dental decay.

The people of this Swiss valley lived mainly on raw, unpasteurised milk and dairy products from their own cows, grazing on the steep mountain pastures. These traditionally-produced dairy foods were supplemented with a little meat, plus vegetables grown in the local terraced gardens. The local diet was high in fats. But they were natural fats, rich in fat-soluble vitamins like A, D and E. They were also rich in polyunsaturated fats including omega-3s and the anti-cancer compound CLA (conjugated linoleic acid).

The foods of the valley were produced on farms, but not the sort that we're used to. They were farms dedicated to producing the kinds of food that human beings had thrived on since they were hunter-gatherers.

The American couple went on to visit remote peoples all over the world. They included Scottish islanders; Inuit communities whose diet was almost entirely made up of animal products; cattle-herding people in Africa who lived exclusively on beef, raw milk, offal meats, and – in times of drought – blood. They visited tribes of hunter-gatherers in northern Canada, the Florida Everglades, the Amazon rainforest and Australia.

Wherever they travelled the couple found these remote populations to be in good health. The foods they ate were, without exception, natural and unprocessed. There were no preservatives, colourings or additives; no refined oils or hydrogenated fats; no processed foods such as white flour or skimmed milk. Nor was there added sugar, though a number of peoples ate naturally sweet foods such as honey or maple syrup. All the foods were grown or raised on fertile soils, uncontaminated with pesticides or chemical fertilisers. Milk and dairy products were always consumed in their raw, unpasteurised state.

Price published his exhaustive findings in his classic book, *Nutrition and Physical Degeneration*.[18] But by then the world was at war and no one took much notice, either in America or in Britain. If they had, a lot of today's disease misery might have been avoided.

To live long and healthy lives, Price discovered, human beings needed the traditional foods of the countryside, including animal products with their natural fats. As many doctors were discovering from their work overseas, it was western processed foods that were at the root of the emerging disease epidemic.

The message today is that, wherever we live, our farmlands are quite capable of delivering the foods that will make us healthy. The farming methods that once protected our health can begin to heal us today if we let them. Doctor and nutritionist Natasha Campbell-McBride believes our best – perhaps our only – protection against the tidal wave of degenerative disease is to return to real food; the kinds of foods Weston Price wrote about in the mid-20th century.

Campbell-McBride trained in Russia where she practised as a neurologist. After starting a family she moved to the UK where she became interested in nutrition and particularly in its role in treating common physical and mental illnesses. Having taken a second degree in nutrition, she opened her own clinic to help children with behavioural and learning disabilities, and adults with digestive and immune system disorders. Her natural food treatments are now offered by trained practitioners around the world. The conditions they help with include autism, dyspraxia, allergies, attention deficit disorder, dyslexia, depression and schizophrenia.

The common factor in all these conditions is some abnormality of the digestive system. The gut is where most human immunity is located. It comes from the huge colonies of beneficial bacteria that reside there, our gut flora. Processed foods damage these microbial protectors, allowing pathogenic organisms to gain control. Without the healthy gut flora to protect us, toxins pass through the gut wall into the bloodstream, where they cause both physical and mental harm.

Natasha proposed the term Gut and Psychology Syndrome (GAPS) for the underlying disorder that leads to many chronic conditions. She treats both adults and children by changing their diets, putting them back onto pasture-fed meat, fish and shellfish, offals (especially liver), non-starchy vegetables, fruit and nuts. In short, the natural, unprocessed foods that human beings have been eating for thousands of years. When people return to these 'heritage foods', modern chronic conditions often disappear.

Natasha's book *Gut and Psychology Syndrome* has now sold hundreds of thousands of copies around the world.[19] She has trained more than 800 GAPS practitioners to help sufferers, both adults and children. She has also written on heart disease, explaining what she sees as the true causes of such modern scourges as heart attacks, angina, high blood pressure, strokes, arrhythmias and vascular disease.[20] Once more the principal cause is the foods we eat – or rather the processed fake-foods we eat, especially those high in sugar and refined flour. And once more the remedy is real food, the traditionally-farmed foods from a fertile countryside.

I first met Natasha when she agreed to speak at a farming conference I was helping to organise in Oxford. Most of the audience were farmers. Some were large-scale growers of wheat and sugar beet. With great passion she laid out the facts. The fields that surrounded her home were mostly devoted to the very crops that were making the nation ill. Given the audience it was a brave stance. But she sat down to enthusiastic applause, even from the arable farmers. They, too, are victims of our dysfunctional countryside.

Some time later I visited her on the small Norfolk farm she runs with her husband Peter. In a county known for its large arable farms, this small corner of Britain was an oasis of beauty and wholeness. There were vegetable plots, a small orchard and soft fruit areas all carefully laid out. But most of the land was down to flower-rich pasture, the domain of goats, ducks, chicken, geese, and ginger Tamworth pigs. On that bright day in early summer there seemed to be birds and butterflies everywhere.

This is how easy it is to grow healthy foods. No giant machines are required. No vast animal factories. No sprayers or chemicals. No lorry loads of animal feeds filled with chemically-grown grains. We could fill Britain's countryside with farms like this and halve the cost of the NHS practically overnight. Isn't it what the countryside's for?

Fortunately, amid all the devastation created by modern, industrial farming it's still possible to find farms producing the right foods in the right way. What makes them special is that they rely on the ancient gift of pasture, the living carpet of grasses and flowering plants that still drapes most of our hills and valleys.

By reintroducing grass-fed foods into our diets we could, in one easy step, make a huge improvement in our nutrient intake. We could begin to recover the levels of strength and fitness enjoyed by our hunter-gatherer ancestors. Perhaps this sounds rather too good to be true. You're probably thinking these grass-fed foods are likely to be pricey. Fine for the well-off, maybe, but beyond the budgets of ordinary working people, especially when there are children to feed.

However, in my view these grass-fed superfoods ought also to be super-affordable, especially when bought direct from the farmer. While producing meat and milk at nature's pace inevitably takes longer than the starch-fuelled methods of the factory farm, pasture farmers have fewer expenses. The energy comes from the sun, fertility from the living communities of the soil. No chemicals, expensive buildings or gas-guzzling machines are required. What's good for us is good for the countryside too.

Later we'll discover how to find these foods and give them a regular place in our meal schedules. But first let's take a closer look at the part they could play in making the world a healthier place.

CHAPTER 2

How grass makes you healthy

Born in the years following World War Two, the baby-boomer generation had a lot going for them. Unlike earlier generations they didn't get sent off to war. Their university education was paid for by the state, and for graduates and non-graduates alike there were plenty of jobs on offer.

But perhaps the greatest advantage of all has gone unnoticed. The baby-boomers were the last generation to grow up on real foods – grass-fed foods. For as long as there have been humans occupying this land we call Britain, we've eaten the meat of grazing animals. For the past 5,000 years or so we've also drunk their milk, or made butter and cheese from it. Throughout our history these foods were the basis of the nation's diet. No one questioned their nutritional benefits.

Today we eat meat and dairy foods from animals fed on grain, not grass. This would have seemed extraordinary to past generations – the idea of taking wheat and other edible grains and feeding them to livestock. Yet a good deal of our meat, together with most of our milk and dairy foods, comes from animals and poultry eating large amounts of starchy cereal grains.

These dumbed-down versions of traditional foods, together with processed foods containing wheat flour and sugar, have brought in their wake a host of chronic, degenerative diseases. This is no great surprise. It's exactly what many doctors and scientists predicted when we started out on this path more than half a century ago.

Among them was nutritionist and academic Dr Hugh Sinclair, who directed the Oxford Nutrition Survey during World War Two. His job was to collect data on the diets of different groups in society, from pregnant women to manual workers. From these he attempted to establish links between diet and disease. As part of his work he got the chance to compare the health of hunter-gatherers in northern Canada with that of air force pilots.

He found there were big differences, particularly in the build-up of cholesterol in various parts of the body. He measured these deposits in the skin, the arteries, and in the eye – in the cornea and in the lens where it formed cataracts. He was astonished to find there were no cholesterol deposits in the native peoples, not even in the elderly ones. But among the young pilots – all of whom had been selected for their fitness and for eating what were considered healthy diets – one in ten showed cholesterol deposits.

Earlier as a young student, Sinclair had quizzed his teachers about why – despite the many advances in medicine – so many people in middle age were succumbing to chronic degenerative diseases such as cancer, heart disease and rheumatoid arthritis. Why, in the more privileged countries of the world, he asked, did a middle-aged man have a life expectancy only four years longer than a century earlier? In Scotland life expectancy was actually decreasing.

After the war Sinclair returned to Oxford University and started looking for answers. In an article in the *British Medical Journal* of December 1957 he wrote that the most likely cause was a deficiency of essential fatty acids. These are the unsaturated fats including omega-3s and omega-6s that the body needs but cannot make for itself. They have to be supplied in the diet.

Sinclair found that these fats were key to protecting people against conditions like heart disease, lung cancer and leukaemia. He showed that the processing of foods almost always reduced their levels of essential fats along with those of vitamins E and B6, which were needed to make the fats function efficiently. He became highly critical of the growing farming practice of feeding starchy grains to cattle, sheep and pigs.

Today farmers feed far more cereal grains to their livestock than ever before. Much of the meat eaten in western countries comes from factory farms or CAFOs – concentrated animal feeding operations. Large numbers of animals are crowded together in sheds or yards and fed grain-rich, starchy diets. Like human beings on similar diets, they get fat.

Because they're kept in such unnatural conditions they're also likely to be hit by infectious diseases, so they often need to be treated with antibiotics and other medicines. As hunter-gatherers we feasted on animals that were inherently healthy. Today the animals we eat are likely to be unhealthy.

The people who run today's livestock industries know all this. Yet they perpetuate the myth that the way animals are fed and managed has no effect on the nutritional value of our foods. They'd like us to believe that beef is beef, lamb is lamb and milk is milk however they're produced. The way farmers feed their livestock is their own business, they argue, and nothing to do with consumers.

It's an argument the industry won't be able to sustain for much longer. The evidence is becoming too strong that changes to farming have altered the composition of many everyday foods. Instead of protecting our health they're now contributing to the diseases that currently fill our hospitals, just as Sinclair warned half a century ago.

In December 2013 a research paper was published in the online scientific journal PLoS ONE. It focused on the nutritional quality of organic milk. The study – which involved both American researchers and scientists from Newcastle University – looked at the fat content of both conventional and organic milk sampled from dairies across the United States. Of key interest were the relative proportions of omega-6 fats and omega-3 fats. These are the essential fats Hugh Sinclair was so concerned about in the mid-20th century.

The results of the US study on milk are so striking that they ought to change our whole attitude to this basic food. As Sinclair understood, omega-3s and omega-6 fats are both needed by the body in small amounts. But what seems most important is that they occur in the diet in roughly equal proportions. If one of them is consumed in greater amounts than the other, things start to go wrong.

Over the past few decades the proportion of omega-6 fats in western diets has increased dramatically while the level of omega-3s has slumped. This is because we've all been advised by nutrition experts to replace animal fats such as butter and lard with vegetable oils. Traditionally animal fats came from livestock grazing pasture, so they were rich in omega-3s. Many of the vegetable oils we've replaced them with are high in omega-6 fats. This fundamental change in the proportions of the two fats may have set people in western industrial societies on a path to disease.

Inside the body both types of fat are incorporated into the membranes of every cell. Cell membranes play a crucial part in metabolism, partly because they control the flow of materials in and out of the cell, but also because they determine the activity of enzymes and of cell messengers known as prostaglandins, which regulate a wide variety of body functions.

Within the cell membrane omega-3s and omega-6s are largely interchangeable – evolution has made them this way. In nature, omega-3 fats are chiefly found in green plants and grasses, while omega-6s are found mostly in seeds. For man the hunter-gatherer this meant that summer-time diets were higher in omega-3s, with omega-6s becoming more plentiful for a short period in the autumn.

According to Susan Allport, author of *The Queen of Fats*, this cyclical change in the occurrence of the two fats helps prepare humans for the season ahead. When cell membranes contain useful amounts of omega-3s, metabolism is rapid and the body is prepared for activity and reproduction. When seeds are abundant – and more omega-6s are incorporated into the structure of cell membranes – enzyme activity slows down.

As Susan Allport puts it, the body 'hunkers down', getting

ready for harder times to come. This means laying down extra fat to help the human animal survive through the tough winter period. Unfortunately, with modern western diets, most of us get this seasonal fat ration – with its heavy omega-6 overload – all year round. This is why we feel sluggish and have a tendency to obesity.

This permanent surfeit of omega-6s has an even more damaging effect on health. Prostaglandins – the cell messengers – are made from the polyunsaturated fats in the cell membrane. Those made from omega-6s are more likely to produce an inflammatory response in tissues than those made from omega-3s. Inflammation is now believed to play a part in many chronic diseases including heart disease.

In small amounts omega-6 fats are a vital part of the immune system. But when there are too many of them in the diet they can lead to heart disease, diabetes and a host of other degenerative conditions. According to Susan Allport there's hardly a chronic disease of western nations that isn't linked to the double effects of these two families of fatty acids.[1]

Healthy diets contain roughly equal proportions of the two families so they're taken up in similar amounts for incorporation into cell membranes. In societies with long life spans – such as those in Japan and in some Mediterranean countries – cell membranes are usually found to contain omega-3s and omega-6s in balanced amounts, allowing for the normal seasonal variations.

People on modern western diets – with their high content of omega-6s – need to find rich sources of omega-3s to restore the balance. This is why they're sometimes advised to eat large amounts of fish. This isn't necessarily a good idea, particularly for pregnant women. Fish often contain heavy metals and other contaminants, so the consumption of more than one or two portions a week isn't recommended.

Changes in farming have made matters worse. Half a century ago most dairy cows and beef cattle grazed fresh pasture in the summer. In winter they were fed large amounts of hay or silage (preserved grass). This feeding pattern produced milk with relatively high levels of omega-3s.

Today many farmers have switched their cattle from traditional grass-based diets to what they call 'total mixed rations' based on grain, maize and soya. This has led to a fall in the omega-3 content of milk and meat, and a rise in omega-6 levels, resulting in a less healthy ratio of the two fats. By contrast organic farmers have stuck to a more pasture-based system of farming, so it's thought their milk ought to be better for us. This is what the American researchers set out to discover.

The results were dramatic. Averaged over a full year, organic milk contained 25 per cent less omega-6 fatty acid and 62 per cent more omega-3s than conventional milk. By substituting full-fat organic milk for conventional or skimmed milk, consumers could significantly lower their risks of heart disease, diabetes, obesity and violent behaviour, said the researchers. In an earlier study, higher levels of omega-3s in the diet were found to be as effective in reducing heart disease risks as taking statin drugs.[2]

The American findings are particularly important for pregnant women and their babies, and also to infants and children through to adolescence. Researchers warn that when the balance is shifted too heavily towards omega-6 fats, the developing foetus becomes more susceptible to a range of neurological and immune system disorders. The scientists conclude that consuming full-fat organic milk is a practical means of cutting the risk factors for a wide range of developmental and chronic health problems.[3]

What seems to matter is how much fresh grass there is in the animal's diet, whether or not the diet is organic. Omega-3 levels in organic milk are generally higher because under the rules of organic production farmers must supply at least 60 per cent of the cow's diet in the form of grass or forage. But the organic label is no automatic guarantee that the milk will be good. Within the rules, organic farmers are still free to feed large amounts of cereal grains to their cows. The fact that these grains are organically grown won't stop the milk having the wrong kinds of fat.

This is why – organic or not – farmers running their herds on pasture for much of the year are likely to produce the best milk, at least in terms of these health-protecting fats.

If you're concerned about diet and health it's obviously an important study. Following its appearance in the online journal, the *New York Times* ran a feature article on the issue. In the UK the *Daily Mail* gave the findings good coverage. But there's been very little media coverage since. The dairy industry – which has a heavy investment in systems for housing cows for much of the year, and feeding them on grain-based rations – isn't keen on the message getting out.

The meat industry seems as determined as the dairy industry to keep the pasture connection secret. During my time as a farming journalist I was invited to an open day at a leading agricultural research centre in the West Country. There I learned about new research showing that lambs reared on moorland pastures, containing a wide range of different grasses and herbs, produced meat that was packed with health-protecting nutrients – omega-3s, CLA and vitamin E. Not only was this meat far healthier than the meat from lambs fed on grain, it was more nutritious even than lamb from grass alone.[4]

Many years later I'm still waiting for the story to hit the mainstream media. The meat industry perpetuates the fable that what animals eat has no significant effect on the nutrient content of the meat. It's the industry's big secret. But the truth is that it's of vital importance to all of us. Grass and not cereal grains hold the key to good health.

Omega-3 fats are linked to photosynthesis and are formed in the green leaves of plants and in ocean plankton. This is why seafoods are a rich source. But they are also found in the meat of grass-fed animals. Cattle and sheep fed mainly on fresh grass produce meat with up to two-thirds more omega-3 fatty acids than animals fed grain-based diets. Unfortunately, when these animals are taken off pasture and transferred to grain diets, the level of omega-3s falls quickly.

Omega-3s are not the only health protector that grasslands have to offer those who eat meat and dairy foods. Conjugated linoleic acid – CLA – is an omega-6 fatty acid with powerful health-promoting properties. It was discovered almost by accident by researchers at the University of Wisconsin. They had been studying various foods, looking for cancer-causing compounds produced by cooking.

Instead they found CLA, which is now known to be an effective cancer-fighter. It has also been shown to protect against heart disease, diabetes and obesity. The compound is present in large amounts in the meat and milk of animals grazing fresh pasture,[5] but when even small amounts of grain are introduced into the diet, the levels in food drop dramatically.[6] In an investigation into levels in milk, cows getting their entire ration from grazing pasture were found to produce milk with five times more CLA than cows on conventional, grain-based rations.[7]

The more lush the pasture, the greater the amount of this health-promoting compound ending up in the meat or milk. On average the fat of Irish milk contains up to three times more CLA than the fat of American milk, which is mostly produced from housed cattle fed on grains.[8]

Even modest amounts of CLA can have a big impact on health. One researcher estimated that eating a single serving of grass-fed meat a day – plus a portion of cheese and a glass of milk from a grass-fed cow – can significantly reduce the risk of cancer.[9]

Most dairy foods made from the milk of grazing cows contain high levels of CLA. This includes butter, yoghurts and many types of cheese. Beef, lamb and other meats from grazing ruminant animals are also rich in the compound. Even turkeys running on pasture are able to produce the compound from fatty acids in their diet.

While all pastures put CLA into the meat and milk of grazing animals, traditional, herb-rich pastures produce the biggest amounts, exactly as they do with omega-3 fats. CLA is produced in the animal's rumen by the action of microbes on simpler substances found in the leaves of plants. While grasses contain good levels of these compounds, they occur in much larger amounts in the leaves of wild plants such as dandelion, knapweed, cat's-ear, ox-eye daisy, plantain, rough hawkbit, self-heal, bird's-foot trefoil, clover, sorrel and yarrow.[10]

A century ago almost all Britain's grasslands contained this rich diversity of wild species. It was these flower-filled pastures that inspired generations of poets and artists. Country people also knew they produced healthy foods.

Today most of these ancient pastures have gone, victims of the modern farming fashion for 'clean' grassland – single-species monocultures getting heavy doses of chemical fertilisers. Many more have been ploughed up to make room for the big arable prairies now growing cereal grains, oilseeds and sugar beet.

Grass-fed foods have many other benefits in addition to a healthy fat profile. Cattle grazing pastures incorporate up to ten times more beta-carotene and up to five times more vitamin E into their muscle tissues than grain-fed animals. Beta-carotene – which is converted to vitamin A in the liver – and vitamin E are fat-soluble vitamins known to be vital for health.[11]

Dairy cows grazing fresh young grass produce milk with high levels of the fat-soluble vitamins, A, D, K and E. Butter made from this milk is a particularly rich source. Today many health experts ignore the role of fat-soluble vitamins in preventing heart attacks, mainly because they're in animal fats. In current medical orthodoxy these are still deemed to be unhealthy. Yet it has long been known that fat-soluble vitamins protect against heart disease, cancer and infections.

In the mountain areas of Britain, village peoples had a deep respect for the health-promoting properties of their butter. For centuries it was the custom of communities on the northern and western side of the country to take their cows up to the high mountain pastures in summer. This was the milk they made their butter from.

Today, research shows that butter from these flower-rich summer grazings contains a range of health-protecting nutrients that are either absent, or present at far lower levels, in the same foods from grain-fed cows. It's almost impossible to find this healthy butter today. Popular brands often carry meaningless phrases such as 'traditionally churned'. What they don't give you is the information you really need – is the milk used to make it from grass-fed or grain-fed cows?

One honourable exception is the Irish brand Kerrygold. The pack states that it's made from the milk of grass-fed cows.

⋙⋘

It's not just cattle and sheep that deliver a health bonus from pasture feeding. Virtually all food animals benefit from regular access to fresh grassland. Eggs from pasture-raised hens provide an array of health-protecting nutrients. Compared with the eggs of caged, grain-fed birds, genuinely free-range eggs contain higher levels of B vitamins – particularly folic acid and vitamin B12 – considerably more omega-3 fatty acids, plus higher levels of vitamins A and E.

Free-range birds are also less likely to be infected with salmonella, the bacterium responsible for most cases of food poisoning. A UK survey showed that no less than 25 per cent of farms with caged birds tested positive for salmonella. In free-range flocks less than 7 per cent of farms tested positive, while in organic flocks the figure was below 5 per cent.

The benefits of pasture-feeding apply as much to table birds as they do to egg-layers. Birds raised on fresh grassland contain more B vitamins, more carotenes – especially lutein and zeaxanthin – and more omega-3s than intensive broiler chickens. What's more, exposure to the sun ensures their fat will be richer in vitamin D. The more yellow the fat, the more nutritious it'll be.

In their TV shows both Hugh Fearnley-Whittingstall and Jamie Oliver urged viewers to pay a little more for their chicken and to buy only free-range birds. In doing so they'd help put an end to the inhumane conditions under which caged birds were raised, the chefs claimed. They might have added – but didn't – that an end to these conditions would be as beneficial for us humans as for the wretched factory chickens. Freeing the birds would lead to healthier lives for people, too.

However, the full nutritional and health benefits apply only to pasture-raised poultry. When it comes to chicken, the term 'free range' is much abused. It can simply mean allowing birds onto the same piece of muddy, pecked-over grassland day after day. This will do little for the health of the birds or for the health of the people who consume them.

Chicken manure is high in nitrogen. In grass – if there's any left on the over-stocked patch of land – it produces a bitter-tasting forage that the birds don't want to eat. Moving the chickens' mobile house to a new patch of fresh grass at regular intervals keeps the ground clean and gives the birds continuous access to nutritious, leafy greens.

It seems the benefits of pasture for turkeys are even greater than for chickens, mainly because they forage over a wider area. They thrive on the green plants and the insects in the pasture, producing meat that – unlike chicken – is high in cancer-fighting CLA.

Even pigmeat is healthier when it's from animals reared on pasture rather than shut in sheds and fed mostly on grain. Sows raised on grassland have more vitamin E and selenium – a powerful antioxidant – in their milk than grain-fed animals. These higher levels of nutrients appear in the meat of their offspring.

What all this evidence adds up to is that moving farm animals from their traditional pastures, confining them to sheds and feeding them on grain-rich diets has had a deleterious effect on our health. The unintended consequence has been to rob diets of health-protecting nutrients and fuel the near-epidemic of obesity and degenerative diseases in western industrial nations.

Down through the ages, the foods of grazing animals have been highly prized as nutritious and healthy. When I was growing up on a Reading council estate in the early 1950s, pasture-fed foods made up a large part of our diets. Almost all our meat came from grazing animals. Cheap, grain-fed poultry meat was virtually unknown.

Beef appeared regularly on the table. When I played out in the street on a Sunday morning with my little gang of mates, the smell of roasting beef seemed to envelop the whole estate. We ate it hot on Sunday, cold sliced on Monday and minced in cottage pie on Tuesday. All our beef came from the Co-op butcher at the top of the road, and much of theirs was sourced in Argentina.

It would certainly have been pasture-fed, probably on the pampas, the great prairie grasslands that stretched from the River Plate in the north to Bahia Blanca in the south, and west to the very foothills of the Andes. Then, as now, Argentina produced some of the world's finest beef.

Our butter came from another great grassland region, New Zealand's famous Canterbury Plains. There the pastures – with their rich mix of grasses, herbs and fertility-building clovers – were grazed all year round, making the milk and butter that came from them genuinely free-range.

From time to time lamb would appear on the table. Some of this would also have come from New Zealand, with the rest from our local pastures in Berkshire. Either way it's a safe bet that it would have been entirely pasture-raised.

The one food I knew for certain to be local was our milk. Each morning the milkman delivered three pints of 'silver top', the badge that declared it to be the ordinary stuff as opposed to the higher-fat 'gold top', the product of Jersey and Guernsey cows. Even though it had a lower fat content the thick band of yellow cream stretched a good way down the bottle. In those days skimmed or semi-skimmed milk was practically unheard of.

Our milk came from a local dairy that had been set up by a Berkshire farmer before the war. Like many dairy farmers of the inter-war period, he had been so incensed by the low prices paid by the big dairies that he started up his own milk round. By the time my brother and I had arrived to squabble over who got 'the top of the milk' on his breakfast porridge, this enterprising farmer was supplying half the town.

While I've no idea how that dairy herd was run, it's likely the cows would have spent a lot more time grazing fresh pasture than most herds today. There were other foods from grass, too. Some of the eggs my mother bought in the local shop would have come from hens in mobile chicken houses moved regularly across a grass field, allowing the birds constant access to fresh pasture. Even our Christmas pork is likely to have come from outdoor pigs rootling around in the turf.

With the memory of wartime shortages still fresh in people's minds, the foods we ate were principally the foods of grassland. The idea that animals should be fed large amounts of grain would have seemed scandalous. Not many years earlier, when U-boat packs hunted the Atlantic seaways, thousands of merchant seamen died bringing in the wheat that would produce our basic ration of bread.

Fed to cattle, it takes about 8 kilograms of cereals to produce just a kilo of beef. Raising meat this way would have looked like a criminal waste of good food and an insult to the sailors who had given their lives on the convoys.

Besides, most people were perfectly happy with their everyday foods. Apart from wartime horrors such as dried egg, most foods tasted pretty much as we wanted them to taste. And, unlike today when many people are confused about which foods are good for them and which aren't, everyone knew their ordinary staples to be healthy and nourishing. And though the national diet was higher in saturated fat than today, levels of heart disease and cancer were far lower.

⋙⋘

To get Britain back on a healthy track it's clear we need to reinstate our traditional foods, especially those from grasslands. This means releasing animals and poultry from their barns, compounds and cages, and putting them back onto herb-filled pastures as nature intended.

The last time I saw fields like this was on a walking holiday in the Jura – the French side of the limestone plateau that runs parallel to the Alps. Wherever we went the pastures seemed to be full of herbs and wildflowers. And I don't just mean the rough hill pastures. We saw plenty of species-rich grasslands like this in the more fertile fields close to the smartly-maintained farmhouses.

Quite a few of the plants I recognised. I spotted yarrow, plantain, silverweed, vetch, dandelion, bird's-foot trefoil, hawkweed, clovers – both red and white – scabious and gentian. Along with these familiar plants were a number of others I didn't know. They obviously weren't in the pastures by accident. They'd been sown deliberately. And it didn't take us long to find out why.

This was the home region of Comte cheese, considered by a foodie friend of mine to be one of the finest cheeses in the world. We ate a lot of it on that holiday. It has a sweet, nutty taste with lingering flavours that give it real depth. In the French Jura you see it everywhere – from cafés and truck-stops to the top *hôtels gastronomiques*.

The rules for producing it are strict, and they start right there on the farm. Milk producers are not allowed to use nitrate fertilisers, nor are they permitted to feed their red-and-white cows any fermented feeds, which means silage is out. The cows are virtually free-range – they stay out on the pastures for much of the year. The farmers don't even bring them in for milking. They milk them in the fields through mobile milking parlours called bails. Back in the early 20th century these were widely used in parts of Britain, particularly on the southern chalk downlands and on the low-lying pastures of the Somerset Levels.

In the Jura, dairy farmers have stuck with pasture farming – despite the availability of cheap grain – because it produces a superb-tasting cheese that everyone wants to buy. And though cheese connoisseurs might not realise it, the chances are they're getting life-enhancing doses of CLA and omega-3s. Could this be one of the reasons why the French live so long?

I got the chance of a chat with one of the local farmers in the bar of a small hotel where we stayed one night. In the best French I could muster I asked him if he'd ever thought of boosting his milk output by feeding his cows on grain and soya as many British farmers do. He looked at me as if I needed locking up.

'You want me to make an industrial cheese', he retorted, 'when I can do very well producing real food. This way our customers are happy, we're happy and the tourist office is happy. And in case you haven't noticed, the cows are happy, too.'

Coming from the UK it was hard not to notice. The Jura cows – the breed was Montbéliarde, we discovered – appeared sturdy, bright-eyed and alert. Sadly not all British cows are in such fine shape. Feeding large amounts of grain to ruminant animals makes their digestive systems acidic. This leads to conditions such as lameness, infertility and udder infections, all of which are common in today's dairy industry.

There are dangers for consumers, too. Grain-feeding of cattle greatly increases the risk from dangerous pathogens such as *E. coli* strain 0157. It takes as few as ten of these organisms to cause illness, even death in human beings. In the highly acidic conditions of grain-fed cattle the bacteria develop a degree of acid tolerance. This makes them more hazardous to humans since they're able to withstand the acid conditions of our own digestive systems.

Scientists at Cornell University found that when cattle on a grain-rich diet were switched to a grass-based diet, their production of acid-resistant *E. coli* bacteria dropped substantially after just a few days.[12]

Despite the clear health advantages of keeping animals naturally, on pasture, the industry seems intent on concentrating them in ever-bigger herds and shutting them up in sheds. An army of scientists and ruminant nutritionists is employed devising new, cost-saving diets to replace the one nature prepared for them. As a result the nutritional quality of a once wonderful food is further dumbed down.

Keeping animals and birds imprisoned in sheds and cages is life-destroying – for us as well as them. We evolved in a world of movement. Animals move in their ceaseless foraging across grasslands and through forests. We humans are made for movement, too. It's an essential feature of the beautiful world we inherit. When we imprison our animals and feed them unnatural diets it's our own bodies we're cheating.

CHAPTER 3

Our occupied land

If you live in Britain and you eat, the chances are you're consuming a lot of wheat. It's hard not to. I know because I've been trying to kick the habit since I discovered – in late middle age – that it wasn't fats causing my high blood pressure and raised blood glucose and cholesterol. It was the amount of sugar and refined white flour I was tucking away. When it comes to ill health these two are pretty equal in villainy.

Wheat is everywhere in our western food culture. It's in the foods that have become our modern staples – our bread and pasta, pies and pizzas. It's in the foods we nibble between meals, the things we tell ourselves are treats: our cakes, biscuits and savoury snacks. They're the foods that fill the snack cabinets of coffee shops and occupy vast stretches of shelf space in our supermarkets. On the breakfast cereal aisles whole-wheat 'goodness' is hyped up as the ideal way to start the day.

The British countryside, once constructed around the growing of real food, has been redesigned for the production of cheap wheat for food processors. It's a landscape shaped by the so-called 'green revolution' of the Seventies. Novel wheat varieties produced far bigger crops than anything that had gone before. It was the scientific breakthrough that was going to feed the world. The new varieties were the tools that would connect farmers to global markets.

Today the super-wheats are everywhere – on the chalk downs and on the thin soils of the Cotswolds; under the wide skies of East Anglia and the flat Midlands plain; on the rolling hills of Yorkshire and on the Lincolnshire Wolds. Big wheat and its partner crop oilseed rape now dominate the landscapes of Austen and Hardy; of Gainsborough and Constable.

Without serious opposition the countryside has undergone a massive makeover. Farmers have taken to wheat-growing with gusto. Many of them were glad to get rid of their livestock. Animals take a lot of looking after. They demand a 24/7 commitment from farming families, plus high labour costs where skilled staff are employed.

Under the new all-arable system, farmers could delete these costs from their accounts and enjoy an easier life into the bargain. Some now choose to pay contractors to do all the routine work involved in crop growing – the cultivations, the sowing, the spraying and the harvesting. Compared with life on the mixed farm – where there were animals as well as crops to deal with – life seems a lot more straightforward. In the winter months, with little going on in the fields, the family can even head off on a skiing holiday. Fat chance of doing that when there were cattle and sheep to look after.

What no one questioned was the impact of these changes on our diets. The traditional farming landscape with its grass fields and grazing had produced real foods; not so very different in their nutrient composition from the foods humans had thrived on as hunter-gatherers.

By contrast the new landscape of crops doesn't produce foods. It grows commodities like wheat, rapeseed oil and sugar, commodities that will be deconstructed by processors and reassembled into the manufactured products that fill our shopping trolleys. Farmers are no longer growers of foods for people. They're in the business of turning out raw materials for factories.

Like all manufacturers, the food companies want their raw materials cheap. To stay in profit, farmers are under constant pressure to achieve the highest possible output for the least possible cost. They must goad their crops with pesticides and chemical fertilisers to maximise output. As a result the cereals and vegetable oils that end up in our processed foods are likely to be light on nutrients and heavy on pesticide residues.

Is our new-look countryside merely a reflection of our growing taste for processed products rather than our traditional, natural foods? Or have we all been duped into buying them by companies who see an opportunity to turn cheap starch, vegetable oil and sugar into profitable brands? Either way, the open landscapes of industrial cropping reveal a nation in a state of confusion over food.

Thanks to the negative press over animal fats we're now eating less than half the beef we consumed in the Fifties.[1] Lamb consumption has fallen even further. We're eating less than one-third of what we got through in the Fifties. The meat we've taken to in a big way is chicken. Back in 1950 we consumed just 19 grams a week. Now we've been told it's better for us than red meat, so we eat fourteen times more.

However, the chicken we chew in fast-food restaurants

isn't the chicken of half a century ago. It used to be from birds ranging over fresh pasture. Today it's from birds kept in sheds and fed on cereal grains. Science shows the outdoor-raised meat to be rich in healthy omega-3 fats, and to have a healthier balance of omega-6 to omega-3 fats. Today's grain-fed chicken is higher in saturated fat and lower in the more beneficial fats.

Our beef and dairy foods have changed too. The cattle that have disappeared from the fields are now in sheds. There they are fed increasingly on starchy cereal grains, maize and soya. As in poultry, high-energy feeds like this change the nutritional value of the meat. Beef and milk today are higher in saturated fats and lower in essential fats than they were when cattle grazed fresh grass. Whether they're the cause or not, changes in our countryside are linked to poorer diets.

A share of the blame must lie with the experts charged with giving us advice on healthy eating. For many years the UK Food Standards Agency (FSA) has recommended that we 'base our meals on starchy foods'. This is because diets high in fats were wrongly linked to an increased risk of heart disease. So the agency recommended that we cut our fat intake, substituting the calories in starchy carbohydrates for those lost as fats.

The fat theory of heart attacks, the basis of the FSA advice, has now been largely debunked, at least by experts who have studied it seriously. Its architects, writes James Le Fanu, glossed over the fact that the amount of fat in the diet predicted neither blood cholesterol level nor the risk of heart disease in any single country.[2] The great cholesterol deception, as he calls it, was the result of the official endorsement of a false theory.

Back in the 1970s US politicians were coming under pressure to find a solution to the growing number of deaths from heart attacks. Though the numbers were tiny compared with heart disease deaths today, health advisors wanted answers. University physiologist Ancel Keys, who had tried and failed to prove that cholesterol consumption caused heart disease, then attempted to implicate saturated fat. There were other theories around at the time, some far more convincing. One of them was that heart disease was caused by the newest component of human diets – refined carbohydrates, particularly sugar.

But at the time Senator George McGovern wanted a quick political solution to the epidemic. According to Zoe Harcombe, author of *The Obesity Epidemic*, the Keys theory might not have been the only one on the table. There were plenty of scientists arguing that sugar and processed carbohydrates were the main danger. But the fat-causes-heart-disease theory was the best promoted. As a result the US changed its dietary advice in 1977 and the UK followed in 1983.

'We told people that fat was bad and carbohydrate was good not because we knew either fat to be bad or carbohydrate to be good. The only evidence against fat was that, in seven hand-picked countries, heart disease tended to be linked to cholesterol levels, which tended to be linked to saturated fat intake. So heart disease tended to be linked to saturated fat.

'Association was never proven. Causation was never even claimed. Nor was there evidence that carbohydrate was good. But if you tell people not to eat fat they must eat something. So it was recommended starchy carbohydrates replace the fat as an energy source.'[3]

Had the policy-makers bothered to look, they'd have found plenty of evidence that starchy foods are anything but healthy. As long ago as 1869 Thomas Hawkes Tanner, author of *The Practice of Medicine*, wrote that 'farinaceous [starchy] and vegetable foods are fattening, and saccharine [sugary] matters are especially so'. Obesity, diabetes, heart disease, gallstones, dental cavities and gum disease are all closely linked. By the late 1920s American doctors were reporting that a quarter of their heart disease patients also had diabetes.[4]

In 1966 a retired Royal Navy doctor, Surgeon Captain Thomas 'Peter' Cleave, co-published a book called *Diabetes, Coronary Thrombosis and the Saccharine Disease*. In it he and his co-author argued that all the common chronic diseases of western societies – including heart disease, obesity and diabetes – had a single cause, what they called 'refined carbohydrate disease'. Sugar was the primary carbohydrate involved. Starch in white flour and rice is converted into blood sugar in the body. So they opted for the term 'saccharine disease'.

Cleave's argument was that the refining of carbohydrates represented the most dramatic change in human nutrition since the invention of agriculture. Processed foods containing refined carbohydrates were so easily digested that they led to a rush of blood sugar to the pancreas, which was simply overwhelmed. Diabetes was the result. He showed that increased sugar consumption in the UK closely mirrored the rise in deaths related to diabetes.

But such arguments held no interest for policy-makers. They had already decided that saturated fats were the cause of heart disease, even though there was precious little evidence for it. By the late 1970s the fat-causes-heart-disease theory was already being written into textbooks and taught at medical schools. Any scientist who offered a counter-argument risked having his or her career blighted.

Science writer Gary Taubes, author of *The Diet Delusion*, says that in the study of nutrition, chronic disease and obesity there has been a distinct lack of rigorous, questioning science. Practical issues on public health have taken precedence over the critical evaluation of evidence and meticulous experimentation. The result has been 'an enormous enterprise dedicated in theory to determining the relationship between diet, obesity and disease, while dedicated in practice to convincing everyone involved, and the public most of all, that the answers were already known.'[5]

I saw an example of this when I attended a conference on food and health a few years ago. Most of the speakers were professionals working in the field of nutrition and public health. They recited the usual platitudes about the need to get more people onto low-fat foods such as skimmed milk and vegetable oil spreads. But towards the end of the day one brave speaker came up with a counter-view.

Sally Morell Fallon is founder of the Washington-based Weston A. Price Foundation, named after the dentist-turned-nutrition-researcher of the 1930s. The group campaigns for a return to 'real foods' including saturated fats, particularly those found in pasture-fed meat and dairy foods. Fallon told the conference that processed foods rich in sugar, refined white flour and manufactured vegetable oils were the cause of most modern diseases. Her paper unleashed a wave of anger from the healthy-eating professionals.

She was accused of reciting non-scientific nonsense and of confusing the public with her 'bizarre' views. These were simply that people would be healthier if they returned to the naturally-grown, unprocessed foods that human beings had been eating for thousands of years. Hardly a radical proposal. As Gary Taubes observed, the 'healthy diet' movement, while claiming to be a science, functioned more as a religious cult.

Having investigated every single piece of scientific evidence behind the fat-causes-disease theory, Taubes reached what he called 'inescapable conclusions'. They were that dietary fat, whether saturated or not, is not a cause of obesity, heart disease, or any other chronic disease of civilisation. The problem is the carbohydrates in the diet. Sugars – including the junk food industry favourite, high-fructose corn syrup – are especially harmful.

Through their direct effect on insulin and blood sugar, refined carbohydrates, starches and sugars are the dietary cause of coronary heart disease and diabetes. They are also the most likely dietary causes of cancer, Alzheimer's disease, and the other chronic diseases of civilisation, Taubes concluded.[6]

Evolutionary biologist Daniel Lieberman outlines the mismatch between the foods our bodies are adapted to digest and the junk foods we actually give them. As it happens, we evolved to eat plenty of carbohydrates and store them efficiently as fat. But the carbs we evolved to eat are the complex kind contained in vegetables and tubers. We're not adapted to consume them in the modern, concentrated form in which they're found in fizzy drinks, candy bars, cakes, biscuits and all the other industrial foods we enjoy.[7]

Without our noticing it, the countryside has been redesigned to produce the very foods that are filling our hospitals and ruining our lives with chronic disease. And in growing them we are driving out the producers of healthy, real foods, the mixed-farmers with their pastures and grazing animals, the farmers who have served Britain so well.

But it isn't just the diet campaigners who have got things tragically wrong. So have the farming policy-makers and the experts who advised them. On very flimsy evidence they decided it wasn't necessary to include grassland and grazing in a farm rotation for it to grow healthy food. Industrial nitrate fertiliser would do the job just as well. Sadly this has turned out to be a big error. The evidence is written on our damaged soils and contaminated environment.

There's no better place to see the whole destructive process than on Salisbury Plain in Wiltshire. For centuries this gently rolling downland with its big skies and bare hilltops has been dominated by flower-rich chalk grasslands. In Victorian times the farmers found effective and sustainable ways to manage it using the sturdy local sheep. Today the sheep and the grasslands have gone. Much of this land is routinely sown with wheat and subjected to the full barrage of chemicals – nitrate fertilisers, insecticides and fungicides. As a result a good deal of it has now been ruined.

I took a drive along the A303 trunk road across the Plain on a sunny spring day at the end of a long, cold winter. I was heading for Southampton but I had time in hand so I decided to stop at a favourite spot of mine, Yarnbury Castle. It's an ancient earthworks about 3,000 years old. I knew the place well – some years earlier I had lived in a nearby village. So I parked up on a trackway and climbed the steep side of the massive earth circle.

As a protected monument Yarnbury Castle is still covered by the centuries-old grassland. There were no animals up there on that cool spring day but I guessed it was seasonally grazed by sheep and cattle. From the top of the earth wall you get a fantastic view across open farmland. I was shocked by what I saw. Many of the wheat crops looked thin and stunted. They had clearly been knocked back by the cold winter weather. But more shocking still was the state of the land. Many of the fields had broad patches of white. This was bare chalk where the soil had virtually eroded away.

Decades of assault by chemical fertilisers and pesticides had led to the destruction of organic matter, the carbon-containing material that is the vital food source for the army of micro-organisms that give soil its life and fertility. As the microbes have gone so has the glue that through the ages has held these soils together. The farmers who manage these fields are still getting crops off them, but only by spending massively on chemicals.

The costs of all this are now so high that there's hardly any profit left in most years. What keeps the whole damaging system going is the subsidy from taxpayers. Without this, farmers would have to switch to a more sustainable, less costly form of farming.

Let's look more closely at the pesticide sprays that go on a typical wheat crop destined to go into our daily bread or the breakfast cereal box. Even before the crop is planted in the autumn, the land is treated with a long-acting weedkiller designed to linger in the soil and maintain a continuous attack on weed seedlings. The farmer might choose to apply the most widely used of all weedkillers, glyphosate, better known as Roundup. This kills virtually all vegetation. It's a real scorched-earth system.

The seed when it's planted will have been coated with a fungicide to protect it against diseases in the soil. There may well be an insecticide on it too, to prevent damage from soil-living pests such as wire-worm. When the wheat seedlings come through, the serious spraying starts. Often the young plants are treated with a mix of different fungicides. A single chemical is no longer enough because the disease organisms have developed resistant strains, a constant headache in modern chemical agriculture.

There's also likely to be another dose of weedkiller before the autumn's out. And if there's a threat from pests such as aphids or orange wheat blossom midge, the young crop will be sprayed with an insecticide.

The following year the pesticide programme really gets into gear. Between New Year and harvest, the growing wheat's likely to be sprayed at least half a dozen times. To stop fungal disease ripping through the crop it will need a cocktail of fungicides in early March, again late in the same month, perhaps twice more in April, in May and finally in early June.

Weather patterns differ from year to year, so the disease pressure, as it's called, varies. But modern wheat crops are notoriously susceptible to disease.

Then there's the risk of pest damage. When aphids and other insects threaten, another insecticide spray will be required. As if this toxic battery wasn't enough, many farmers now spray their wheat crops with the weedkiller glyphosate shortly before harvesting. The chemical has the effect of drying out the wheat plants, making harvesting faster and cheaper.

Traces of many chemicals end up in our bread, our biscuits, our breakfast cereals and our pizzas. Pesticide contamination of everyday foods isn't some freak event. It's an inevitable result of our food system, adding an additional toxic hazard to processed foods that are already unhealthy. The irony is that most crop pests and diseases would cease to pose a serious threat if our soils hadn't been wrecked by the chemicals.

The usual justification for this kind of industrial crop growing is that it's the only way to feed the world's fast-rising population. But as we'll see later, these methods actually represent a threat to food supplies in the damage they do to soils and the environment. A far more productive way of farming Britain's chalk downlands was developed by Victorian farmers.

Between the mid-1830s and the mid-1870s farming in southern England became increasingly intensive. On the chalk downs, the farmers of Hampshire created a highly intensive form of farming based on growing a wide diversity of crops and keeping large sheep flocks. The system didn't depend on chemical fertilisers and pesticides. Yet even as the output of food increased, the techniques used protected and actually improved the environment.[8]

Instead of sticking with the methods that worked, farmers on the chalk downlands switched to chemical methods. In winter the consequences are visible for all to see. It's a process that isn't confined to Salisbury Plain. The chalk hills of the downs are bare because of water-borne soil erosion and it's happening right across Britain.

The Environment Agency estimates that across the UK more than 2 million tonnes of topsoil are eroded every year,[9] costing £45 million to clean up and causing £9 million-worth of lost production.[10] Across Europe more than half of all farmland shows some degree of water-borne erosion, according to the European Commission.[11]

What none of these reports shows is the impact of degraded soil on our health or the prospect of our farmland being able to feed us in the future. In some ground-breaking research on the American prairies, a team from the University of Colorado has discovered that the switch from grassland to crop growing led to a collapse in the microbial populations that hold the ecosystem together.[12] The team under Professor Noah Fierer used DNA gene technology to study the microbial populations under the prairie grasslands as they existed in the early 19th century, before they were ploughed up for crops.

America's tallgrass prairies once stretched from Minnesota in the north down to Texas and from Illinois west to Nebraska. They were home to dozens of grass species that grew as high as human beings. They also supported hundreds of species of wildflowers and huge herds of roaming bison. The prairie soils that underpinned them were incredibly fertile. This is what caused their destruction. The European settlers found that by ploughing up the grassland and planting wheat they could get bumper crops – for a time. Today the fertility of the land has gone. To grow decent crops of maize, wheat and soybeans, modern farmers have to rely on chemical fertilisers, pesticides and irrigation.

Only tiny fragments of these ancient grasslands still remain, mostly in nature reserves and old cemeteries. The Colorado researchers collected soil samples from them and looked at their microbial make-up. The results showed that their microbial populations were dominated by a poorly-understood group of bacteria known as Verrucomicrobia. It's clear that they were a key to the fertility of that lost grassland ecosystem. It's also clear that the soil microbial populations under today's intensive cropping are very different. But the findings raise worrying questions about what we're doing to the land's future ability to grow healthy foods.

Commenting on the Colorado findings, South African scientists warn that today's farmers may be repeating the mistakes of past civilisations that failed because they degraded their soils.[13] Human health and well-being still depend on fertile soils, and we may be in the process of destroying them.

Modern fertilisers and irrigation systems could be giving us a false sense of security by masking the long-term damage. Will soil microbe populations become so compromised that they'll finally collapse, leaving the land unable to grow anything? Looking at the white streaks of bare chalk on those once-productive Wiltshire soils I couldn't help wondering if we'd already reached this point.

High on those ancient earthworks in Wiltshire I made my own small discovery about this bit of antique grassland. As I strode along the top of the massive earth walls I noticed there were dozens of molehills. In many places there were clusters of little heaps of earth, the burrowing animal's own monuments in the landscape. On many of them the soil looked fresh. After weeks of freezing temperatures, the warmth of the spring sunshine seemed to have sparked a flurry of activity among the mole population.

Out in the cultivated fields it could never have happened. There wasn't enough soil left. In most of them it was scarcely deep enough for a mole to burrow. Even where enough soil remained, there'd have been few earthworms to feed on. Worms are near the top of the subterranean food chain. With the microbial life dramatically reduced, there would have been nothing to support them. Yet under the ancient grassland the soil clearly provided a decent diet for moles, a good indication that the soil life generally was in fine shape.

I took a close look at the soil they'd thrown up in their miniature spoil heaps. It was dark grey in colour, as any chalk country soil is likely to be. But it was crumbly and rich in organic matter, the kind of soil you'd be very happy with in your garden or on your allotment. So out in the fields – despite all our smart technology – we have a wasted landscape, barely able to produce food without massive application of pesticides and chemical fertilisers. But under the ancient turf, soil remains as fertile and productive as it was when the shadowy figures of the past were toiling to build Stonehenge a few miles down the road.

For 3,000 years that ancient turf has been grazed by cattle and sheep. Throughout this time it has produced the healthiest of meats and dairy foods out of nothing but rain, sunshine and grazing animals. Today learned scientists and nutrition experts bang on about food security and the need to produce more from less. They might start by taking a close look at the soils of Yarnbury Castle, and how their microbial populations differ from the soils of our ruined and contaminated arable fields.

Generations of farmers have known that grasslands are a reliable means of producing good food. It's why the grass 'ley' – a short-term grass turf – was used as the main fertility-builder of the productive and sustainable mixed farm. Today this traditional wisdom has been forgotten. Few farmers believe it's possible to grow a good crop without chemicals.

The change of thinking began in the 19th century. If you had to attribute it to one person it would probably be the charismatic German scientist Justus von Liebig. From the time of Aristotle, philosophers had believed that plants were sustained by organic material gathered from the soil. Although this idea had come under attack in the late 18th century, it was von Liebig who finally blew it out of the water.

In a paper to the British Association for the Advancement of Science in 1840 he put forward the theory that plants obtained their carbon, oxygen, hydrogen and nitrogen from the atmosphere, and the other elements they needed from the soil. These essential elements included iron, sulphur and phosphorus in the form of phosphate.

Liebig's theory was wrong. In spite of this, he sparked a radical shift in thinking as he travelled up and down Britain lecturing landowners and selling his own patent fertiliser.

Through the power of his personality he demolished the idea that there was something special about living matter; that it contained some mysterious 'life force'. Farming was simply a matter of calculating the amounts of chemical elements removed in the crop at harvest time, then putting these back on the land as some form of soluble fertiliser.

Extraordinary though it may seem, von Liebig's thinking dominates modern arable farming. Crop growing is still seen as chiefly a matter of chemistry. The idea that the biology of soil might play some major part is barely considered by today's farmers, a mindset encouraged and reinforced by the pesticide and fertiliser manufacturers.

The chemical habit was given a further boost by the brilliant Prussian scientist Fritz Haber. Shortly before the start of World War One he developed a process for getting the two gases hydrogen and nitrogen to combine to form ammonia.

It was – and is – a process requiring huge inputs of fossil energy, mainly natural gas. The synthesis of the two elements will take place only under intense heat and pressure. The resulting ammonia is easily converted to soluble salts such as ammonium nitrate. Haber's process offered the prospect of limitless supplies of nitrate fertiliser at a time when lack of nitrogen was believed to be the chief factor limiting crop growth.

But on its own not even nitrate fertiliser could have brought about the total transformation of food production. One more ingredient was needed – a different kind of crop plant. Enter American scientist Norman Borlaug, winner of the 1970 Nobel Peace Prize for his work on developing high-yielding strains of wheat.

Until the 1970s most wheat plants were tall. This meant that if you put on too much nitrogen fertiliser the stems would buckle and collapse. But in the 1930s Japanese farmers and plant-breeders had produced a short-strawed wheat variety known as Norin 10. At maturity it was just half the height or normal wheat strains.

In the 1960s Borlaug used the Japanese variety to produce a clutch of short-strawed wheat varieties. Some of this genetic material reached Cambridge, where a team of scientists developed a family of semi-dwarf wheats, the first of which was called Hobbit. The new crops had far better 'standing power' than the old varieties. They allowed farmers to apply far higher levels of nitrate fertiliser without the risk of the crop collapsing.

For the first time in Britain's farming history, pasture

and grazing animals were no longer needed to underpin the nation's food supply. Chemicals produced with fossil energy could now out-perform solar-powered grassland when it came to feeding the people. Or so it seemed in the 1970s. Across the world, nitrate fertilisers and the new genetics quickly filled up the grain bins. By the end of the decade even Britain – a net wheat importer for more than a century – was producing a surplus. Much of it was sold off – at taxpayers' expense – to the Soviet Union.

While the miraculous yields of the so-called 'green revolution' tripled worldwide grain production in the second half of the 20th century,[14] we consumers have paid a high price. Though it's not mentioned on food labels, pesticide residues are now regular contaminants of everyday staples, including bread and flour.

The UK government's expert committee monitoring pesticides in foods found that in 2011, 97 per cent of non-organic flour samples contained pesticide residues.[15] In non-organic bread samples, 74 per cent were contaminated with residues. Over a five-year period flour was found to be one of the twelve dirtiest foods when it came to pesticide contamination.[16] Not only are wheat-containing foods playing havoc with our insulin levels, they're making us swallow a wide variety of toxic chemicals.

The pesticide residue that occurs most often in wheat is the weedkiller glyphosate, the most widely used weedkiller in the world. In 2011 it was found in five foods including bread and flour. A group of scientists at the French University of Caen found that the chemical disrupted human sex hormones and could 'induce reproduction problems'. Studies of farmers and others exposed to glyphosate weedkillers have shown increased rates of the cancer non-Hodgkin's lymphoma, miscarriages and attention deficit disorder.[17]

Weedkillers like glyphosate kill plants by stopping them taking up the minerals they need for normal, healthy growth. They're known as 'chelators', which means they form a barrier around essential nutrients like copper, zinc, iron and manganese. All these elements are needed by crop plants for the enzyme systems that protect them from pests and diseases. Farmers use glyphosate on weeds between successive crops and on GM glyphosate-tolerant crops.

Blocked by weedkillers from taking up these nutrients, plants quickly die. Glyphosate is a particularly effective plant killer, which is why it's so popular with farmers. Outside Europe, many grow GM crops engineered to tolerate even higher doses of the chemical, making it even more common in animal feeds and ultimately in human foods.

When I worked as a farming journalist, glyphosate – Roundup – was becoming just about the most profitable weedkiller of all time. Its makers – the biotech giant Monsanto – assured us it was non-toxic. When it hit the ground it was harmlessly degraded, said the company. Right now the claim is looking a little hollow.

Professor Don Huber, an American agricultural scientist, has highlighted some of the risks posed by the chemical. His research, carried out over more than 50 years, has been devoted to how farming systems can be managed to produce better crops and healthier food. He's now convinced that glyphosate poses a serious threat to human health, particularly when used at the high rates associated with GM crops.

In blocking the uptake of essential nutrients like iron, zinc and manganese, he says, the chemical doesn't just affect plants. It has the potential to harm any living organism that needs these nutrients – and that includes human beings. Once in a plant, the chemical can't be removed or washed off. It's absorbed and moved to every part of the plant. This is why residues turn up so regularly in wheat flour and bread.

In safety tests glyphosate has always been considered harmless to humans because it disrupts a metabolic pathway – the shikimate pathway – not found in mammals. However, the pathway *is* present in the bacteria inhabiting the human gut, which play a vital part in maintaining health.

Dr Stephanie Seneff, a research scientist at the Massachusetts Institute of Technology, argues that glyphosate residues found in some of the common foods in the western diet – including wheat – 'enhance the damaging effects of other food-borne chemical residues and toxins in the environment to disrupt normal body functions and induce disease'.[18] This is linked to most of the diseases associated with western diets including gastrointestinal disorders, obesity, diabetes, heart disease, depression, autism, infertility, cancer and Alzheimer's disease.

This is the hidden threat within those tempting cakes, biscuits, muffins and flapjacks in the cabinets of our favourite coffee shops. If they're not labelled as organic they're very likely to contain these unwanted extra ingredients. And when you buy any of the thousands of wheat products on offer in the local supermarket, you won't find glyphosate or any of the other common residues mentioned on the ingredient list.

Chemical wheat growing is promoted by biotech companies as the best way to feed a hungry world. In reality it's turned out to be one of the biggest threats to human health and food security. What's scarcely believable is that we continue with such a damaging system when we clearly don't need its product.

The five-year average for UK wheat production is a little over 15 million tonnes.[19] Just over one-third is turned into foods for human consumption, the processed products that are probably making us ill. Another 40 per cent is fed to animals to produce meat that is far less healthy than the grass-fed meats we all used to eat. The rest, about one-quarter, is either exported or turned into biofuel.

Biofuel production – carried out under the EU's Renewable Energy Directive – is the latest idea for propping up the price of wheat, even though, by any reasonable estimate, we're producing a vast surplus. Britain's two major plants turning wheat into bioethanol have a combined capacity for 2 million tonnes of the crop. The biggest – the Vivergo plant near Hull – is owned and run by the agribusiness giant ABSugar, the oil company BP and the pesticide and biotech company DuPont.

Here's a clue, surely, to why our most productive land is locked into such a ludicrous and damaging system for growing wheat. It makes big profits for global corporations, especially those trading in fossil fuels, pesticides and chemical fertilisers.

For the rest of us it's a near-total disaster. Fortunately there's a safe and proven alternative – pasture.

In the early 1950s – when Britain had scarcely shrugged off wartime rationing – a team of researchers embarked on a 30-year experiment to compare the sustainability of producing food from grassland and from cultivated crops.[20] The researchers – from the now-defunct Grassland Research Institute in Berkshire – studied what happened to soils under grazed pasture and under farmland that was cultivated every year for arable crops.

At the end of the experiment the organic matter content of the intensively-cropped soil had fallen by a third, even though it had been at a low level to start with. The soil now contained a little more than 1 per cent organic matter. The upper soil layers had become so hard that any crops they grew were highly susceptible to drought. Without their annual fix of chemicals they'd have been incapable of producing anything.

However, the soil under pasture showed a steady rise in fertility. A huge population of earthworms showed that it was in a far healthier state than the cultivated land. What's more, the organic matter levels in the soil had risen by more than half in the first ten years, equivalent to an annual increase of more than a tonne of soil carbon to every hectare.

It's one of the extraordinary gifts of grasslands that, even as they produce more food, the fertility of their soils increases so they have the potential to produce even more. As if this weren't glorious enough, the nutrient content of those foods grows, too. Year by year, carefully-managed pasture farms turn out more food and healthier food, while at the same time enriching the soil and safeguarding the food supply in years to come. It comes as close as anything could to delivering the elusive 'free lunch'.

Isn't it time to abandon the 50-year experiment in chemical grain growing and put pasture back into our field rotations? We'll grow less than half the wheat we grow today, but it will be richer in nutrients and free of pesticides. We'll have no need to grow vast amounts to feed to animals in sheds because most of our meat and dairy foods will come from animals living naturally in the open air on grass.

We'll be returning to the mixed farms that were our heritage and that we should never have abandoned. Not far from where the 1950s researchers carried out their studies on grassland, one young farmer is creating just such a farm.

I'll never forget my first visit to Kingsclere Estates, if only because it was so cold. We stood in the middle of a frozen crop field near Basingstoke in Hampshire. It was typical of the local arable farmland – open and windswept with few hedges or blocks of woodland to break it up. A bone-chilling north-west wind blew across the field. It was a March day towards the end of a long, cold winter. Things ought to have been warming up. But I've never felt so cold in all my life.

Tim May, the young farmer whose land we were on, had more to worry about than a cold wind. This field on the family farm ought to have been covered in the green shoots of a growing wheat crop. But there were no green shoots. The land was almost bare. Through the cold winter days the autumn-sown crop had become steadily weaker. There were no signs of any particular disease. Instead the young plants slowly lost their vigour until at last they gave up the struggle.

For Tim this came as a serious financial blow. The crop would have to be replanted at considerable expense. Along with the cost of cultivating the land and preparing the seed-bed, there would be extra seeds and chemicals to pay for. But before the field was replanted with a spring-sown cereal, Tim needed to find out why the first crop had failed to thrive. His money was on a weakness in the soil. On some sloping fields deep fissures had opened up as topsoil had eroded away in the winter rains.

To get to the root of the problem, Tim hired a mini-digger and excavated a deep slit-trench in the middle of the field. He called in leading soil and crop expert Mike Harrington to take a look. The sidewalls of the trench gave a clear picture of the 'soil profile' – the various soil layers. Together, farmer and soil expert climbed down into the trench to see what was going on.

Harrington is a soil enthusiast. He's fascinated by them. He spends his working life sampling them, studying them, analysing them, digging his hands deep into them, rolling small bits of them around in his hands. He knows soils in all their states and conditions, in all their moods and in all their stages of life. As a soil fertility consultant, his livelihood depends on keeping them in good shape. For the past twenty years farmers have paid him to help them manage their soils and produce good crop yields from them.

But in that cold Hampshire field he was in something of

a quandary. As well as being a soils specialist, he's an agronomist. They're the people who advise farmers which chemical to spray next in order to keep their crops free of pests and diseases. As well as collecting fees from farmers, agronomists often pick up commissions from pesticide companies.

This is why Mike had a problem. He has become increasingly worried that the chemicals no longer work. In fact he now believes it's the chemicals themselves that are causing soils to collapse. They're destroying the very ecosystems that enable farmland to produce healthy crops. Far from increasing our food supply, they threaten us with sickness and, ultimately, hunger.

In that Hampshire field Harrington soon diagnosed the problem. On top of the orange-brown layer of subsoil deep down in the trench there was an upper, dark-brown layer about 30 centimetres thick. This was topsoil, the biological powerhouse where much of our food is made. On this field it didn't look particularly healthy. Mike dug around with his trowel. The soil appeared solid and impenetrable. No channels or air-spaces were visible. There wasn't much chance of a plant root breaking through this solid mass, let alone an earthworm.

In a quiet, matter-of-fact voice the soil expert delivered his verdict. The topsoil was dysfunctional and probably had been for years. It was only able to grow a crop at all because of the large amounts of chemical fertiliser and pesticide sprays that had been applied. These had at least allowed the plants to survive and grow.

But for the farmer it's an expensive way to produce food.

And for the rest of us who are destined to eat foods from fields like this, it's a recipe for long-term illness. Crops grown this way are unlikely to deliver their full complement of nutrients. They're also likely to be liberally laced with pesticide residues.

Harrington has seen dozens of fields like this in the past few years. He believes it should come as a wake-up call to all of us. 'When we started on this way of farming we all assumed the chemicals would work alongside the natural, biological processes of the soil', he says. 'But it's now clear that the natural systems are collapsing. Without them the chemicals don't work. It's the chemicals that are the problem.

'Throughout our history we've fed ourselves by methods that keep large amounts of carbon in the soil. Returning plant and animal wastes to the land as compost; spreading animal manure on the land; keeping grazing animals on pasture. All these are ways of putting carbon back into soils. In other words we were feeding the soil microbes. Carbon kept our soils healthy and productive. Now the carbon's gone and so has the life of our soils. We're all in deep trouble.'

The discovery that this was happening on his Hampshire farm came as a shock to Tim May, who runs the family-owned Kingsclere Estates. But with three young children he's not about to ignore it. In his lifetime he has seen the livestock and most of the staff disappear from the farm he grew up on. There used to be a dairy herd and a pig herd as well as arable crops. Tim remembers when there were 28 people working on the farm, and at one time there were no fewer than 44.

Like most lowland farms at the time, it still practised mixed farming. Grassland and grazing kept up soil carbon levels and built the fertility to ensure the land stayed productive year after year, decade after decade.

But over recent years the thousand or so hectares at Kingsclere had been entirely sown to arable crops, heavily reliant on chemical fertilisers and pesticides. The farm was run by just three people, Tim and his team of two staff. Everything had been done in accordance with the best cropping practices. All the rules and codes of practice on chemical use and soil protection had been followed. Even so, the soils eventually broke down under the strain.

Now Tim has made the brave decision to return to mixed farming. After more than fifteen years livestock are back on the Hampshire farm. So are grazing pastures. The aim is to put new life into his exhausted soils. Tim has planted half the land with what he calls herbal leys, pastures with a wide range of grasses, clovers and deep-rooting herbs. He has brought in a large sheep flock plus a sizeable herd of cattle. He's counting on grazing to restore his damaged soils to new life.

Instead of selling commodity grains, he has begun selling nutritious, pasture-fed meats, the foods that the people of these islands have been eating for thousands of years. No longer will the farm be plugged in to global markets. The aim now is to produce nutrient-rich foods for the people of Hampshire and surrounding counties.

Tim admits the change isn't without its financial risks. The economics of today's agriculture favour industrial crop production. But for the sake of his young children he wants to give his farm a long-term, not just a short-term future.

How long it'll take for the rest of Britain's arable farmers to follow Tim's lead is anyone's guess. But a change in our eating and buying habits will speed the process. Just by making sure the meat and dairy foods we eat are from animals grazing pasture, we'll help put life back into the countryside. By choosing the healthiest foods for ourselves and our families we can begin to return our land and our planet to health and new life.

CHAPTER 4

A landscape for life

If you believe the supporters of modern, industrial crop growing, the world is headed for a food crisis. Put at its simplest, populations are rising and crop yields are falling. Unless something changes we face a grim future of hunger, conflict and despair.

What's needed, say the gloom merchants, is a farming system that produces more from less – one that grows more food while using up less of the world's resources like water, soil and fossil energy.

As it happens, we already have such a system. There's a picture of it hanging in London's National Gallery. It was painted by the British artist Thomas Gainsborough in the year 1750. It shows a well-to-do young couple called Mr and Mrs Andrews. They're posed beneath an oak tree at the edge of a cultivated field.

The couple look rather pleased with themselves – as well they might. He's a successful banker. She's the daughter of one. He stands nonchalantly beside his wife, a shotgun under his arm, an adoring spaniel at his feet, his tricorn hat tipped at a rakish angle. She wears a fine silk dress and sits on a rococo-style bench. They have the self-assuredness that often comes with land-ownership.

Some art buffs have suggested that Gainsborough was taking a satirical poke at his clients. He's known to have had a hearty dislike for the upper classes. But what's interesting to an old farming journo like me is the glimpse he provides of the north Essex countryside in the mid-18th century.

More than half the picture is given over to 'landscape', a subject Gainsborough would far rather have spent his time on than portraits, or 'face paint', as he called them. These he was bound to undertake for the money. But whenever he got the chance he painted landscapes. And with 'Mr and Mrs Andrews' he shows us a landscape of agriculture.

In the foreground is a newly-harvested wheat field. The neat, parallel rows of wheat stubble show this to have been a thoroughly modern farm. It already uses Jethro Tull's amazing new seed drill. But beyond the distant hedge there's a field of grazing sheep, while in the extreme left of the picture you can see cattle grazing in an orchard. Gainsborough's picture is as much a portrait of the English countryside as it is of the Andrewses.

What it shows is the classic mixed farm, the farm of childhood picture books, with some fields sown to pasture for grazing animals and others growing crops for human consumption. In 1750 it represented a new, highly productive system of agriculture. It marked the start of what became known as the agricultural revolution.

Through the Middle Ages British agriculture had relied on resting or 'fallowing' the land as a means of maintaining fertility. For two years a field would be sown to a crop like wheat or barley. It would then be rested for a year. No crop would be sown, allowing the soil to rebuild its fertility through the action of soil microbes. The mixed farm system, which introduced grazing instead of fallowing, produced a quantum leap in output and helped feed a fast-growing urban population. Without an earlier agricultural revolution, Britain's industrial revolution probably couldn't have taken place.

Now let's fast forward nearly 200 years. In the early months of World War Two a whole new set of images were recorded of the British countryside. They were taken by Hitler's air force, the Luftwaffe. They'd been ordered by the Führer to step up their aerial reconnaissance of Britain. Spy-in-the-sky surveillance had been going on since the mid-1930s, mostly using civilian aircraft. Now a more comprehensive scrutiny was required. The High Command wanted bombing targets. They also wanted detailed maps for use in any future invasion.

Under bright summer skies, Heinkels and Dorniers began criss-crossing Britain at a height of around 10,000 feet. Flying in daylight, their crews needed to keep a sharp eye open for RAF fighters. But down in the bomb bays the cold, unblinking eyes of Carl Zeiss cameras remained firmly fixed on the ground. For the German intelligence chiefs who planned the flights, the main objects of interest were military – army camps, aerodromes, fuel dumps, communications centres and the like. However, the images captured by the cameras recorded something far more valuable.

During the summer and autumn of 1940 tens of thousands of pictures were taken by the enemy aircraft. At the end of the war most of them fell into the hands of the Americans, who promptly classified them as secret and stored them away in the US National Archives. Over the years the restrictions have been slowly lifted, and some now appear on commercial websites. The glimpse they provide of Britain in the not-so-distant past is extraordinary. For anyone interested in food and health it's also very disturbing.

The Luftwaffe pictures are astonishing in their detail. They show every hedge, every pond, every copse and often every tree. Together they reveal a forgotten and beautiful land on which the history of a pastoral people was written on the surface. It was a countryside of small fields bounded by ancient hedgerows and interspersed with woodland, scrub and marsh.

Often these miniature fields were gathered around a village or hamlet like chicks around a mother hen. Where there was a town they spilled almost into the streets.

It was an intimate landscape where the fields – like the cottages and farm buildings – were constructed on a human scale. To someone used to modern landscapes of large, open, featureless fields it must seem unreal. Yet to the people who lived in this land every field, every hedge, every patch of woodland had its purpose and its meaning.

To the RAF pilots who (like my father) took to the skies to defend this island, the landscape must also have seemed timeless. It had hardly changed in centuries. In *The History of the Countryside*, Oliver Rackham writes that except for urban expansion almost every hedge, wood, heath and fen recorded by the Luftwaffe photos in 1940 were to be found on the large-scale Ordnance Survey maps of 1870.[1] Much of the wartime landscape would have been recognisable to Sir Thomas More, he says; and some even to the Emperor Claudius.

The reason the landscape hardly changed for more than 200 years was that it didn't need to. It met the requirements of the British people admirably well, producing healthy foods by methods that were entirely sustainable. Most of the output of the mixed farms that made up much of the countryside was in the form of animal products – grass-fed meat and grass-fed milk from cattle and sheep grazing on fresh, flower-filled pastures.

Many pastures contained a wide variety of clovers and herbs. So the animals could graze selectively, choosing those species that would supply the nutrients they needed. Under this kind of farming the soil remained fertile and high on organic matter. This ensured a vibrant underground population of microbes, essential for plants to be able to take up nutrients. These were then passed on to grazing animals, ensuring that they too stayed healthy.

It was a pattern of farming that, in many ways, mirrored the forest ecosystems in which humans flourished as hunter-gatherers. The endless hedgerows that bounded the small fields provided the equivalent of forest grazing for the livestock. Grazing animals don't just eat pasture plants. In nature they will browse on tree vegetation, too. The permanence and deep roots of hedge species meant they were rich in trace elements. As a result they made an important contribution to the nutrition and health of the animal.

This is why the landscape of small fields, pasture and grazing animals persisted for so long. At its best it provided modern humans with the nutrient-rich foods they had thrived on in the ancient forest ecosystems.

Today that landscape of health has been largely destroyed. Many of the hedges have been bulldozed out, while most mixed-species pastures have been ploughed and replaced with single-species grass monocultures. Across large stretches of the lowland countryside there are no pastures of any kind, and no grazing animals. From field boundary to wide field boundary, the countryside has been turned over to the large-scale, industrial production of crops, mainly wheat and oilseed rape.

Most of us think of western agriculture as a success story. Today's farmers feed twice as many people as they did before World War Two. With sophisticated machinery and the latest farm chemicals they produce vast amounts of food with an ever-dwindling labour force. Never in the nation's history has so much wheat poured into the grain silos.

Yet, as we've seen, people are suffering ever more chronic disease. Though we're living longer, it takes a massive medical intervention to keep us going, particularly in our later years.

Our countryside is as sick as we are. Wild species are disappearing and our damaged soils are eroding at an unprecedented rate. Maybe our modern, high-tech farming methods aren't so wonderful after all.

In 2008, in one of the biggest studies ever undertaken of modern farming systems, scientists from around the world concluded that industrial crop growing would not feed the world. It was unfit for purpose.[2] Funded by the World Bank, the study involved more than 400 scientists and development experts.

What was needed, the scientists argued, were 'ecological' methods of farming. There needed to be a broader mix of crops and animals and an end to crop monocultures, along with all the chemicals needed to prop them up. In effect the scientists were calling for a return to something like the traditional mixed farm. In direct opposition to the agribusiness lobby, the scientists saw the abandonment of grazing and the mixed farm as a disaster.

Whatever possessed us to get rid of a national resource that had served the people so well? At the start of World War Two there were almost half a million farms in Britain including part-time holdings. Many were small, mixed units of less than 50 acres, with cattle, sheep, pigs and poultry as well as some crops. They had survived through the tough years between the wars when there were few state subsidies. In uncertain times, growing a range of products gave farmers greater security.

As well as farmers there were almost 1 million workers employed wholly or partly on British farms. So in total 1.5 million families were able to make a living from the land. Without state subsidies they supplied the country with nutrient-rich food crops and grass-fed meat and milk. Environmental benefits came as a 'free' extra. Never has the countryside looked so good. Never has it supported a richer diversity of wild species.

As it happens, I went to work on one of a dwindling number of mixed farms at the end of my student days. Cutting-edge that Dorset farm certainly wasn't. To his farming neighbours the farmer – let's call him Bill T. – was politely known as a 'traditionalist'. In many ways his farm had barely changed in a century. There were pasture fields, filled with clovers and flowering herbs as well as grasses. And in all but the coldest winter months they were stocked with grazing cattle and sheep.

Cereal crops – barley, wheat and oats – were mostly sown in the spring. This meant that for a good part of the winter the stubble fields would be thronged with feeding birds. There were root crops, too – usually turnips – grown as feed for the animals. All these different plants and animals took their allotted places in a seasonal dance that had changed little in centuries.

The reason Bill stuck to the old ways wasn't that he didn't know any better. He would look over the hedge with interest as his neighbours tried out the latest chemical sprays or the new bit of equipment recently featured in *Farmers Weekly*. But looking beyond the hype he seldom saw anything that would make his farm work better.

He operated a system that had stood the test of time. It produced the kinds of foods that had always been considered healthy – grass-fed beef and lamb along with wheat grown with few pesticides on fertile soils. Equally important, in most years it gave him a decent profit. What more could any farmer ask?

For Bill the best part was not having to spend money with the powerful companies supplying agriculture. His farm was largely self-sufficient. He seldom needed to splash out on chemical fertilisers or commercial animal feeds. His own farm supplied all he needed. If a rep called round hoping to pick up a big order for nitrate fertilisers he invariably got short shrift.

What powered Bill's farm were his lush, green pastures and the grazing animals that 'harvested' them. A field would be cropped with cereals for two or three years, then sown down to pasture, or 'clover leys' as Bill called them. These would be grazed by the cattle and sheep for a couple of seasons, during which time the soil would regain its strength. Then the field would be ploughed up for cereals once again.

The cropping pattern had barely changed since Bill's grandfather, a successful local butcher, had bought the farm during the depression of the 1920s. Nor had the field layout. Neither Bill nor his father had followed the post-war fashion for enlarging fields by bulldozing out hedgerows. Some of the hedges were centuries old and contained a great variety of plant species. All were rich in wildlife, especially birds.

If you asked Bill why he hardly ever changed his farming system he'd simply say it wasn't broken. Each year there'd be new crops of lambs and beef cattle. The cereal crops could be relied on to produce a decent enough harvest to fill the grain bins. And since they required little by way of chemical fertilisers and pesticides, the costs were low and the margins high.

Under the age-old cropping pattern the land never became exhausted, though with its thin, drought-prone soils it could hardly be considered prime farmland. Growing two or three cereal crops in successive seasons took a lot out of it. But under pasture and grazing the fertility quickly returned. It was timeless practice that had been known by British farmers for centuries. And that was good enough for Bill.

Not long after I left the farm and went to work for *Farmers Weekly* I heard that Bill had given up. I later discovered that the farm had been sold to an insurance company who promptly got rid of the animals and the pasture. The land was sown down to cereal crops from boundary fence to boundary fence.

The UK was about to join the European Common Market, as it was then called. The generous subsidy payments promised under Europe's Common Agricultural Policy were about to unleash a new round of wheat-growing mania. They would also strike a further blow against traditional, grass-fed foods, which had been under attack since the dark days of World War Two.

With the opening of hostilities in 1939 the government took full control of agriculture. British farming was effectively run by the 'War Ags', the War Agricultural Executive Committees, as they were called. These local committees had enormous power. They could tell farmers what to grow and how to grow it. What they told many farmers to grow was wheat. Thousands of acres of grassland were ploughed up, and over the six years of war Britain's wheat output doubled.

Many large farmers wanted this policy to continue after the war. The increasingly influential National Farmers' Union (NFU) lobbied hard for an undertaking from the politicians that they would bring in public subsidies on the major farm products. These would almost certainly lead to a further expansion of wheat growing.

But there were powerful voices arguing for a different future, a grass-fed future. Among them were a group of influential scientists including the charismatic George Stapledon, the leading agricultural scientist of his day. Stapledon and his colleagues urged that Britain's food production should be based on grassland.

For Professor Stapledon the traditional mixed farm provided all the essentials of a successful food system.[3] First, it maintained the fertility of the land year after year, decade after decade. So long as these islands went on receiving sunshine and rain, farms like this would go on producing good food. Equally important, it made farmers pretty much self-sufficient.

They had no need of chemical fertilisers or imported animal feeds. When times were tough and incomes fell, they could hunker down and wait for things to improve. Overheads were low so they didn't need to borrow money or build big debts. When prices bounced back – as they always did – they could enjoy the good times again.

This is how thousands of small family farms managed to survive through the lean years of the Twenties and Thirties without subsidies from the taxpayer. Stapledon might have added – but didn't – that the mixed farm produced very healthy foods. Most foods from the mixed farm were animal products – grass-fed beef, mutton and lamb; grass-fed milk, butter and cheese; poultry meat and eggs, often from birds roaming over species-rich grassland.

The distinguished scientist probably thought this wasn't worth even mentioning. In the mid-20th century foods like beef, lamb, milk and eggs were universally believed to be healthy. In fact they were known as 'protective foods' since, unlike starchy foods such as bread and potatoes, they were understood to protect the human body against degenerative disease.

As the war approached its end another powerful voice was added to the clamour for a grass-fed future, that of a celebrated farmer called George Henderson. George's book, *The Farming Ladder*, had been the surprise bestseller of 1944. It told the story of two London-born brothers – George and his brother Frank – who rented a small, worked-out Cotswold farm in the early Twenties, just when farming was entering its deepest recession of the 20th century.

The brothers weren't troubled by economic downturns. They were confident that traditional mixed-farming methods would make their farm a winner. They were right. By the start of World War Two – with Britain facing mass starvation as a result of the submarine blockade – their little farm had one of the highest outputs per acre of any farm in Britain.

So impressed were Ministry of Agriculture officials that they bussed in hundreds of other farmers to show them how land should be farmed. In his bestselling book, George Henderson attributed their farming success to the productive power of grassland. He wrote that when he and his brother took over the farm, the land was in such a poor state they knew they'd have to bring in large numbers of cattle and sheep. Only grassland and grazing would restore life to the land by building up the unseen populations of microbes. And only then would fertility return to guarantee bumper wheat crops in the future.

George's book ran to a dozen editions and sold over 100,000 copies. It was mostly bought by young servicemen and women who dreamt of running their own small farms after the war. George wrote that this would be by far the best outcome for the nation. 'If all of Britain were farmed this way', he wrote, 'our country would be easily able to feed a population of a hundred million people. All we'd have to import are bananas.'

What George and his brother Frank had pioneered was intensive farming. But it was intensive farming based, not on chemical fertilisers as now, but on fertile soils and the microbes that inhabit it.

Here was the answer to the jibe that traditional mixed farming was unproductive. Back in the 1930s George Henderson and others proved it could be both highly productive and sustainable. It was to take the world's scientists another 70 years to confirm what this farming pioneer had shown on his few Cotswold acres.

Many years after George's death I visited his widow Elizabeth at the same small farm he had made famous during those wartime years. She, too, had a heroic story to tell. As a young worker in the Women's Land Army she'd been given George's book for her nineteenth birthday. She was gripped by its simple message – that anyone applying the sound techniques of traditional mixed farming could make a good living on the land. She wrote to the author and asked for a job. Within a year the two were married – the nineteen-year-old Land Army girl and the 40-year-old farmer-author. Together they had five children.

As we talked in that sunlit farmhouse kitchen she told me about the spirit of optimism that swept through the countryside in those early years of peace. The idealism that put the new Labour government in power also energised Britain's village communities. After the privations of war, the British people held farmers in high esteem. With thousands of young service people coming home to repopulate the countryside and run family farms, this was surely to be a new golden age for agriculture?

But the optimists had failed to take account of the ambitions of an interfering state. Many, like George Henderson, had wanted the government to remove all controls after the war so farmers could go back to being masters of their own destinies, free to stand or fall by their own decisions.

In response to the NFU's call for subsidies, George warned that these would be disastrous for British farming. He was convinced they would take away all initiative and self-reliance from farmers, creating a 'dependency culture'. At the same time they'd give faceless bureaucrats control over what foods were produced and which methods were used to produce them. There'd been enough of that sort of control in the war years.

Sadly, George and his fellow campaigners for farming freedom lost the debate. Farm subsidies were introduced on a big scale in 1947 by the same government that gave us the National Health Service. Ironically it's the ill-health caused by the mistaken introduction of the new food system that today threatens to bankrupt the health service.

After the years of shortages the post-war political leaders wanted to boost the supply of food. But in doing so they destroyed a countryside created to produce healthy food and turned it into a landscape of waste, exploitation and corporate greed. What the Third Reich had failed to do, the politicians achieved with full public support.

It would be hard to overstate the warm feelings British people held for farming in the post-war years. In the autumn of 1941, after just two years of war, Britain's leader Winston Churchill had given farmers and farm workers a hearty pat on the back. He told them: 'Never before have you responded to the country's call as you have in the past two years. It is due in no small measure to the efforts you have made, in spite of many difficulties, that we find ourselves in a better position on the food front than at any previous time since the war started.'

It's a sobering thought that today's farmers would no longer be capable of responding to such a national emergency. Without huge imports of fuel oil and energy-rich fertilisers and pesticides they couldn't maintain present levels of production, let alone produce more. What the wartime farmers had on their side was a resource seldom mentioned outside geography books.

When they answered the nation's call and ploughed up their land for wheat crops, they knew that, even without imported fertilisers, the soil would contain all the necessary plant nutrients to ensure a good crop. Their soils were highly fertile – a rich store-house of nutrients with crop-growing potential. It was almost as good as having wheat safely stored in the barn. The chief reason for this life-saving bank of fertility was that, until then, farmers made full use of grassland, the crop that had laid the foundations of the nation's wealth and prosperity centuries before.

As country people have understood for generations, grassland provides a truly secure source of food. Cereal crops can fail, victims of drought, storm, flood and tempest. Well managed grassland will survive all such natural disasters and provide a secure food supply.

Unlike cereal crops, pasture-fed foods are genuinely home-grown. To grow wheat crops farmers must now buy in chemical fertilisers, pesticides and fossil fuels, most of which have to be imported. Clover-rich pastures need no inputs, not even nitrate fertilisers. They create their own fertility. And, once they're ploughed up, they bequeath that fertility to the arable crops that follow. That's how the wartime grasslands could be so easily switched to the growing of wheat for the nation's bread.

Foods from grassland are the only foods that can truly be called 'local'. They're grown from the natural fertility of the local soil, not from chemical fertilisers produced in the gas fields of Kazakhstan. Imports can be disrupted. Financial systems can collapse. But our pastures are always there, always local, always producing food down the end of a British lane.

The community's connection with 'the local farm' was strong where I grew up in the early Fifties. We lived in a council house on the northern outskirts of Reading, the first post-war social housing to be built in the town. From the end of our street the gently rolling countryside stretched away towards the Chiltern Hills. Many people on the estate felt a strong bond with it and the farms it supported.

At hay-making time a dozen or more residents could be relied on to help local farmers pitch up the bales onto trailers, then stack them up in the barn. These were working people who'd been busy all day in the office or on a factory floor. But in the evening they'd think nothing of cycling out to a nearby hay-field to spend a further four hours or so in hard physical work.

They didn't expect payment for it. Perhaps the farmer would stand them a quick pint in the local before closing time. But they were pleased to do it because of their feelings for the countryside and the chance of some fresh air. There was also a desire to support a group they generally liked and admired. This was a time when *The Archers* was pulling as big an audience as *EastEnders* or *Coronation Street* draw today. Farmer and writer Arthur Street was a regular panellist on BBC radio's *Any Questions*.

Not surprisingly, a political consensus emerged that farmers, who had helped to feed the nation during hostilities, should not be abandoned with the coming of peace. However, there was no clear agreement about what sort of agriculture the country needed.

George Stapledon, the agricultural scientist, campaigned for the return of the traditional mixed farm. During the war thousands of acres of pastureland had been ploughed up to grow wheat. Now Stapledon wanted the nation to return to grass, her first and greatest source of wealth.

With the support of taxpayers, mixed farming based on temporary pastures ('leys') spread rapidly across lowland Britain. At the height of the pasture-farming boom in the early 1960s, the area of land under 'temporary' grass leys was double what it had been during the depression years before the war.

Stapledon intended his grassland revolution to give the nation healthy foods while at the same time bringing economic revival to the countryside. He dreamt of a prosperous countryside – revitalised by a thriving agriculture, and supporting a growing population. To him the land was a great unifying factor in national life.

Sadly his utopian dreams were dashed. Public subsidies for agriculture led, not to the thriving community of small farms he had hoped for, but the emergence of large predatory holdings that began swallowing up their smaller neighbours.

The main problem for the new breed of career cereal growers was how to stop the price of this swelling tide of grain collapsing as the supply outstripped the people's ability to consume it in bread, biscuits and pies. There was an obvious solution, one used by American farmers when a glut of grain from the former prairie grasslands threatened a price crash. Why not 'add value' by feeding it to livestock – effectively converting grain into meat?

Today grain feeding is everywhere. While few British farmers now house their cattle all year round, many feed them large amounts of unhealthy grains in place of grass. Poultry and pigs are often kept in confinement. Unless they are officially labelled as 'free range', almost all chicken, eggs, pork and bacon are from animals kept in confinement and fed mainly on grains.

It's true these factory methods can produce a lot of cheap protein and fat, but they are 'dumbed down' foods, depleted of the many health-protecting nutrients that grassland once put there. In his book *The Way of the Land*, George Stapledon warned that the abandonment of grassland and mixed farming would lead ultimately to disaster.[4]

But by now farmers were starting to dismantle the countryside so many people loved. Under the inducement of subsidies they mobilised to increase production – as if the war were still going on. They made their fields bigger by bulldozing out hedgerows. They put on more chemical fertilisers and ploughed up old meadows, many with a rich range of wildflower species.

Production was all that mattered. The subsidies meant that the more you produced the more you got paid. So the farmers who prospered were the ones who grubbed out most hedges and used most chemicals. Whatever the cost of all this activity, the taxpayer would foot the bill. Schemes for picking up the cash became ever more ambitious.

In the early Fifties *Farmers Weekly* ran a story about the Dorset farmer who had declared war on his local wood. 'From woodland to wheat', ran the headline. The story that followed told how a farmer near Cranborne Chase had used high explosives and Sherman tanks to clear ancient woodland from his farm. The article's short on detail, but it seems to have been some sort of *blitzkrieg* against the ancient oakwood.

The wood had stood undisturbed since pre-Roman times. But in an operation that sounds uncannily like what's happening to the Amazonian rainforest today, the farmer used jungle clearance techniques to bring the land into wheat production so the subsidies could be claimed. *Farmers Weekly* praised the operation. It was typical of the work being done by 'progressive' farmers along the chalklands of southern England.

With all this extra money coming in, many farming families bought new cars or carpets for the living room. This didn't suit the politicians. They wanted the money spent on more production. To the delight of chemical companies, there were special subsidies for using chemical fertilisers. A 'ploughing-up' grant was introduced to encourage farmers to get rid of flower-rich meadows and replace them with modern grasses.

Later there were grants for grubbing out hedges and for uprooting old orchards. There were grants for draining land. At the peak of all this frantic activity no less than 100,000 hectares of land a year were being drained at public expense. In the beautiful upland areas like the Lake District and the Yorkshire Dales there were extra-large grants on offer for ploughing up species-rich hill grasslands.

Our membership of the EU in the early 1970s further ratcheted up the public subsidies to farmers. Direct payments from the taxpayer were now to be augmented by a hidden tax on food. While the European Community closed its borders to imports, the prices of home-produced foods were inflated by the removal of surpluses from the market, the notorious Intervention buying system. Prices soared and farmers put the last remnants of their flower-rich meadowland to the plough. And still farm ministers urged higher production. The butter mountains rose. The grain mountains grew. And Britain's wildlife was choked, poisoned and crushed into submission.

Modern industrial agriculture has taken a heavy toll on our wildlife. One study of arable land concluded that half the characteristic plant species, one-third of insect species and four-fifths of bird species had been lost.[5] Among the cornfield plants that went into decline were cornflower, corn marigold and red hemp nettle. Along with the wildflowers went huge numbers of beetles, spiders and butterflies. Grain-eating birds like the linnet, grey partridge and corn bunting were also in trouble. So were many mammals like the harvest mouse.

Where grasslands survived, the old meadows and pastures were replaced by the new grasses, heavily fertilised and increasingly cut for intensive silage production rather than hay as in the past. This hit ground-nesting birds like the skylark and the lapwing. The mass removal of hedges took a heavy toll on mammals like the weasel and dormouse as well as dozens of species of butterflies, beetles and bees. At the same time land drainage was making things hard for birds like the redshank, curlew and snipe.

In the early Seventies, while all this rural mayhem was happening apace, I went along to a Saturday afternoon lecture by the writer and conservationist Dr E.F. Schumacher. Clutching my much-loved copy of *Small is Beautiful*, which I later got him to sign, I heard him outline the three goals that he thought should guide the way we manage the land. They were health, beauty and permanence. If we got these things right, he argued, good food would flow naturally from them.

Sadly his words have gone unheeded. Today's farmers are locked into an unending battle with nature. It's a choice between conserving wild species and feeding the world, they tell us; between biodiversity and food production. The people who work the land can be nature wardens and park-keepers, or they can be feeders of growing populations. They can't be both. Schumacher believed this to be a false and dangerous choice. But farmers have stuck to it, and, in doing so, have inflicted great damage upon the countryside.

Food production by monoculture has become the global standard and Britain's once beautiful countryside has been reshaped to accommodate it. Modern cereal growing is concerned solely with quantity; with yield; with the size of machinery needed to extract even more grain from damaged and toxic soils. Except where small corners of the landscape can be ransomed by special environmental payments from the taxpayer, it's a war on the life of the countryside, whether that life takes the form of working people, hedgerow birds or soil microbes.

Despite the prevailing culture, mixed farming based on the productive power of grassland still survives in places. A few brave farmers somehow manage to swim against the economic tide. It's they who are our main hope for a healthier future.

From the higher fields of John Turner's farm at Little Bytham in south Lincolnshire you can look across to the village with its cluster of houses and handsome church tower. All around are tall hedges and flower-filled pastures grazed by fine looking cattle. It's a scene that is quintessentially English. Only the passing of a high-speed train on the nearby East Coast Main Line reminds you that you're in the 21st century.

These particular hundred or so hectares have been through many of the upheavals that have shaken the rest of Britain over the past half-century. In the 1930s, when John's grandfather took over The Grange, it was a very traditional mixed farm. He ran a dairy herd using the local Red Poll breed of cattle, and he grew a wide variety of crops including sugar beet.

By the mid-Sixties the traditional system was coming under strain, John recalls. Mechanisation had resulted in the loss of staff, and by the time his father took over, the subsidy system had begun to operate against mixed farming. In fact under the EU support system of the 1980s, proper crop rotations were impossible to operate. If you wanted to pick up your subsidy you had to give up real mixed farming.

John and his brother Guy have changed all that. In the late 1990s they began converting the farm to organic production. They established a new crop rotation designed to keep the soil healthy and productive without chemical fertilisers or pesticides. From now on there were to be three successive cereal crops followed by four years of grazing pastures. As well as grasses these would contain nitrogen-fixing leguminous plants such as magenta-flowering sainfoin, trefoils and purple vetches. There were also to be clovers and deep-rooting herbs such as chicory and lucerne.

Under these mixed pastures the soils have become increasingly fertile. When the Turner brothers started out on their quest to restore mixed farming the organic matter content of their soils stood at around 3 per cent. Not bad by the standards of modern, intensive farming. But nowhere near good enough for them. Their aim is to get the organic content up to around 7 per cent. This isn't likely to take them long at present rates of improvement. Under their species-rich pastures, soil organic matter is increasing by 3 percentage points every four years.

Grazing cattle are a key part of the fertility-building

programme. The pastures are grazed by a breeding herd of 'suckler' beef cows along with their offspring. The animals are fed no grains for the whole of their lives, which means the Turners are able to sell healthy, nutrient-rich beef. And when the super-fertile pastures are cultivated and sown to cereals, they grow good, nutrient-rich wheat and barley without chemicals of any kind.

To John it's been a journey of rediscovery. He has learned on his own land why mixed farming was the default system in Britain before the coming of chemical fertilisers. Its greatest benefit is that it's genuinely sustainable. There's no need for farmers to buy in any animal feeds or fertilisers. Thanks to grasses and grazing animals – and with the help of sunlight and rain – they can produce all they need at home. The farmer is off the chemical 'treadmill' and can take satisfaction from once more being a free agent.

At The Grange it has been a fascinating journey. John reckons that, having made the decision to give up chemicals, it has taken up to nine years to get their soils fully functioning again. He says: 'On heavy clay soils chemicals can remain active for a long time. They can be influencing the biology of the soil long after you've stopped using them. In fact, putting on chemical fertilisers can mask underlying problems with the soil. But you can't get away with it for ever.

'Every year we see our soils getting stronger and more productive. Sometimes in a cold spring the crops can look quite yellow. But we know from experience that when the soil warms up and the microbial population springs back to life, those same crops will green up and flourish.'

The Turners now aim to sell their high-quality foods closer to home. Already some of the wheat from their fertile ground goes to a local stone-ground flour mill. Soon their healthy, pasture-fed beef will be finding new customers in farm shops and with independent butchers. John is a founder-member and vice-chair of a new organisation called the Pasture Fed Livestock Association. Its aims are to help other farmers produce nutrient-rich, pasture-fed beef and to make it easier for the rest of us to buy it.

'We're producing something very good and very special', says John. 'Now we want to get closer to consumers so they value it and know where to find it.' Though he meant by this the fine beef he and his brother are producing, they're also recreating a very special landscape. Looking across the flower-filled meadows and the tall hedges filled with wildlife, I was glimpsing an older countryside, one known and valued by countless generations of Britons down the ages.

CHAPTER 5

The dodgy science that steals our food

In the summer of 2013 Britain's leading farming research station at Rothamsted in Hertfordshire announced an ambitious new programme to make farming more productive. You might think this would mean putting life and fertility back into soils worn out by decades of chemical farming. Or rebalancing the output of UK farms so they produced more of the foods that protect health and less of the stuff that makes us ill.

Nothing so sensible. Rothamsted's bold new initiative was aimed at growing more wheat. More of the crop we already grow so much of that we have to feed half of it wastefully to animals. More of the crop that'll be processed into the products that have given us an epidemic of obesity, diabetes and heart disease. More of the crop whose production is rapidly killing our soils and silting up our rivers.

The research programme is aimed at lifting the average yield of wheat from its present 8 tonnes a hectare to 20 tonnes within two decades. What's telling is that the programme is being run in collaboration with the world's biggest agrochemical company, Syngenta. Wheat growing is a big money-spinner for the pesticide companies. While the programme will have few benefits for consumers – or even for farmers – shareholders in agribusiness corporations are likely to do well.

The so-called 20:20 Wheat programme is one of those creatures so beloved by modern governments – the public-private partnership. This is why the then Science Minister David Willetts was on hand to give the venture his blessing.

Rothamsted was a world-class agricultural research facility, he said, whose work was of benefit to the wider economy and society. The new partnership would bring commercial expertise to the table, helping to turn excellent science into cutting-edge technologies for farmers.

The announcement came on the same day the government unveiled a £160 million strategy to boost farming technology. It would, said the Science Minister, make the UK a world leader in agricultural science. What it wouldn't do, though of course the Minister didn't say it, was give the taxpayers who finance it healthier foods. Nor would it give them a cleaner environment or a wildlife-rich countryside. It wouldn't even benefit most farmers. Most of the rewards would go to the companies supplying them with expensive inputs.

With Britain's soils haemorrhaging and the health service buckling under the strain, the choice of technology as a priority for farming research seems puzzling. But not when you put it in the context of Britain's current farming policy. The speech of Environment Secretary Liz Truss to the 2015 National Farmers' Union conference is illuminating.

In it there was no mention of soil erosion or of the need

to restore farmland fertility. There was nothing in the speech on healthier food, and if you'd been a livestock farmer waiting for something on the benefits of grass-fed foods, you'd have been disappointed.

What the Environment Secretary wanted to talk about was technology. She praised the food and farming industry for its innovation. No fewer than 16,000 new products were being brought to market each year, she reported, more than in France and Germany combined. She congratulated arable farmers for producing the highest crop yields in the world and she praised dairy farmers for pioneering new technical innovations, presumably technologies like robotic milking.

She told the farmers that they could soon start applying for grants from a £141 million productivity scheme designed to put new technology to work. There was encouragement for GM crops and a veiled warning to the EU Commission that they shouldn't expect an easy ride if they went ahead with proposals to ban or restrict the use of damaging pesticides. Any such measures should be 'proportionate and based on science', she said.[1]

Looked at as a whole, the Environment Secretary's address wasn't a speech about farming. It was a speech about the food business. It started with a hymn of praise to the industry that employed one in eight people and contributed £100 billion to the national economy. What she failed to mention was that farming contributed less than 10 per cent of this. Most was accounted for by the food manufacturers and retailers.

Truss's ministry, the Department for Environment, Food and Rural Affairs (DEFRA), likes to present food industry statistics in terms of what it calls gross value added (GVA). This is defined as the value of goods and services produced less the cost of raw materials and other inputs needed to produce them.[2] The figures for 2014 show household spending on food and drink totalled £112 billion. Of this no less than 60 per cent of the value added came from food manufacturers, wholesalers and retailers. Just 9 per cent is accounted for by farmers.

The industry celebrated by government turns out to be the one that processes and trades in manufactured products. And, as we've seen, most of these are unhealthy processed foods made from cheap, industrially-grown raw materials, especially wheat, sugar and vegetable oil. The government's farm policy isn't about promoting healthy foods and diets. It's about promoting the manufacturing industry that does most to damage them.

The government's obsession with technology has been apparent since it linked up food and farming with the UK science base to exploit a promising new market for farming technologies. Two years before the Rothamsted announcement, the government had set out its vision to make the UK a world leader in agricultural technology, innovation and sustainability.[3] It saw big business opportunities in what it called 'agri-tech', the plethora of new gizmos that farmers are being persuaded to spend their money on.

They include high-tech developments in the fields of genetics, satellite imaging, remote sensing, meteorology and precision farming, which aims to target fertilisers and chemical sprays at the areas that need them. Unfortunately none of these technologies can fix what's really wrong with the food system – that it's fast ruining soils and is producing unhealthy foods.

The global, World Bank-funded study of 2008, mentioned in the last chapter, recognised these shortcomings. But the 400 or so scientific experts involved went much further. They pinpointed the fatal flaw at the very heart of our way of growing food. In doing so they presented an existential threat to the big agribusiness corporations and the elected politicians who support them.

Farming works with biological systems of mind-boggling complexity. If global weather systems are hard to forecast more than a couple of days ahead, below-ground changes to soils are a hundred times harder to predict. Even in the early 21st century we know next to nothing about soil, particularly its living processes, the minute-by-minute interactions of an unimaginable number of micro-organisms. What we do know is that these microscopic populations are vital for our food supply, in fact for our whole civilisation.

Agricultural science as it's now done chooses to ignore these complexities. Experiments are done on small, isolated parts of the system, and on the bases of these food policy is made. The full impact of the changes on the entire ecosystem may take years – even decades – to come to light.

Many field trials were done in the second half of the 20th century to show how nitrate fertiliser increased crop yields. So farmers used more and more of it, especially on wheat crops. Soon it became obvious that crops grown this way were more susceptible to insect pests and plant disease.

This is when the agrochemical industry stepped in with a range of new pesticides to keep crops growing. As each new chemical became widely used the target organism would often become resistant, so new products had to be introduced to replace those that were no longer effective. Monocultures of wheat and other crops, the very basis of our food system, have provided an unending source of riches for the chemical corporations.

In her speech to the farmers' union, Environment Secretary Liz Truss praised the industry for achieving world-beating yield records for arable crops. Her comment came shortly after a Lincolnshire farmer was featured in *Farmers Weekly* for having harvested the highest wheat yield ever recorded, an astonishing 16.5 tonnes per hectare, double the national average.[4]

What the Environment Secretary didn't tell her farmer audience – and probably didn't know – was how many toxic chemicals it took to produce that result. Over the full growing season that Lincolnshire wheat crop required four different weedkillers, an insecticide, five plant-growth hormones, and no fewer than twelve disease-killing fungicide chemicals. Residues of many of these chemicals will stay in the wheat flour, so it's not a crop you'd want to end up in your cakes and biscuits, or, if it's fed to animals, in your pork or roast chicken.

More worrying still is the impact of that kind of chemical cocktail on our soils. As well as all the pesticide sprays, the record-breaking crop needed a massive amount of nitrate fertiliser – almost one-third of a tonne of ammonium nitrate on every hectare. It also had to be regularly sprayed with nutrients in a form that could be absorbed through the leaves. The soil was incapable of providing the nourishment the plants needed.

The World Bank-funded study of farming technology identified the risks to soils of chemical crop growing. The researchers reported that these methods had led to the ruin of almost 2 billion hectares of crop land around the world.[5] Far from solving the world's food problems, high-input western methods were the major threat to food supplies. They were destroying fertile farmlands, the world's best hope of averting famine.

The researchers proposed a new system of farming, one they believed would be both more productive and more sustainable. They proposed a switch from western chemical methods to more natural ways of growing food. Farms should have a greater diversity of crops, often with integrated animal or grazing systems. There would be no single 'blueprint' system as with today's industrial monocultures. Instead countries and regions would choose the system that best took care of their own soils. In Britain this could mean a return to the tried and tested mixed farm.

Professor Hans Herren, co-chair of the study and president of the US-based Millennium Institute, had no doubt that the world needed to find a better way to produce food. The present system, he said, had resulted in a billion hungry people with another billion overweight or obese. It had also caused huge environmental damage, including the loss of biodiversity and soil erosion. The cost of clearing up the mess was passed to taxpayers. The only rational response was to reinvent farming to make it genuinely sustainable.[6]

Herren called for a total change in direction for agricultural research. It needed to cater for the needs of sustainable farming, supporting small-scale farmers and the work of women on farms. Despite the hype surrounding high-tech agriculture, the world's smallholder farmers still fed 70 per cent of the global population. To meet the needs of these small-scale producers, agricultural research needed to be funded by the public sector, not large-scale agribusiness corporations.

In western countries, including Britain, Herren wanted to see farm subsidies either abolished or replaced by support for sustainable farming methods. He called for an end to large-scale commodity production, with shorter supply chains between farmers and consumers. Farmers should get a bigger share of the nation's food spending.

These were not messages that would go down well with a UK government ideologically inclined to find business solutions to farming's problems. Still less did they appeal to large agribusiness companies with their powerful influence on British agriculture. But it was Herren's views on GM crops that really annoyed them.

The World Bank study found that GM crops were no more productive than varieties bred by conventional methods. They also had many disadvantages. They reduced the choices available to farmers, said the study report, and they increased the price of seeds. They also locked farmers into environmentally-damaging mono-cropping systems, making them dependent on a diminishing number of seed suppliers.

This conclusion posed an existential threat to the biotech companies. Many recognised that the days of heavy pesticide use were almost over. The damage to soils and the environment was becoming daily more apparent. GM crops would give them an alternative – and far bigger – income stream. At the same time they could be sold to the public as a way of cutting the use of unpopular pesticides.

Herren's proposal that the world adopt ecological farming methods threatened the entire strategy. Here was a group of renowned scientists arguing that pesticides had to go, but that there was no need to introduce GM crops in their place. Sound biology and publicly-funded research would provide healthy food and a sustainable production system. It was an outright challenge to agribusiness power and to a government that believed in new technologies and the private sector.

The government responded by commissioning its own study of farming methods. Known as the Foresight study, it was directed by the then Chief Scientific Adviser Sir John Beddington. His report painted a more fearful picture of the world's future food supply. The World Bank study had concluded that the world's farmers were already capable of feeding everyone on the planet. There was enough food around, but it was being produced in the wrong places by the wrong methods.

The UK Foresight study was far more alarmist. Beddington himself often used the phrase 'perfect storm' to describe the multiple threats posed by rapidly growing populations, water shortages and climate change. And to the delight of the big agribusiness companies, the report saw a much bigger role for new technologies in securing our future food supply.

Unlike the earlier study, the government's Foresight report was widely publicised right from its 2009 launch. Biotech companies and their partners in the publicly-funded research centres sang its praises loudly and in unison. Their message was simple. The world faced the threat of widespread famine in the not-too-distant future.

To guard against this, food producers needed to use 'all the tools in the box', including GM crops. A clutch of top scientists – including the director of Rothamsted Research, Professor Maurice Moloney – wrote a letter to *The Times* urging a relaxation of the regulations on GM crops.[7] Professor Ian Crute, a former director of Rothamsted, called for 'pragmatism' in the food debate, with nothing ruled out. Among the technologies definitely not to be ruled out was, of course, GM technology.

Fronting the campaign for 'sound science' were plant scientists. These are the specialists who do the gene splicing, creating GM crop varieties in both public research labs and those owned by biotech companies. In March 2014, a group of them presented a report to Prime Minister David Cameron arguing that the UK should go it alone and plant GM crops even if the rest of Europe objects.[8]

A couple of days later the *Daily Mail* 'outed' the report's five authors for having a vested interest in promoting GM crops and food. Far from being independent, some were even part-funded by the industry, said the *Mail*.[9]

I once gave a presentation to a group of young plant scientists at Oxford University. I'd been invited to speak about my take on sustainable farming at a postgraduate symposium in the Plant Science department. I'll admit to being nervous, especially when I learned I'd be sharing the platform with leading scientists from the agrochemical company Syngenta and from the John Innes Institute, one of Britain's leading centres for GM research. The postgrad students would be getting a lot of cutting-edge stuff on chemistry and gene splicing. Then I'd have to stand up and tell them that putting pasture and cattle back in the crop rotation would do a far better job for food security.

In the event the students gave me a polite listen. A few of them were clearly interested in a more natural approach to farming. But it's fair to say that most held the view that new technologies would be needed to feed a growing world population. There was also the serious matter of jobs. Since successive UK governments have drastically cut back on public research in farming – preferring to leave it to the private sector, that is, to the biotech industry – most of the jobs for these young plant scientists were going to be with agrochemical and biotech companies.

However, at the end of my talk I discovered that I had one enthusiastic supporter in the room. She was a young research student from China. At the end of the session she came up to tell me of China's thousand-year history of growing food by sustainable ecological methods. In the Mao Zedong era the country had switched to western methods, with disastrous consequences for soils.

Today she and many of her fellow scientists had learned the lesson. They were revisiting the traditional, ecological methods and learning how to apply many of them today. To me this came as a revelation. It seems to be a peculiarly British idea that, as a scientist, you can campaign for any particular technology and call that 'science'.

Back in my days as a farming journalist I worked for an editor who was in the habit of describing chemical-based farming as 'scientific agriculture'. The implication was that farming systems that didn't use chemicals, such as organic farming, were somehow unscientific, even anti-science. But it was the so-called scientific approach that was degrading soils, wiping out wildlife and polluting waterways on an unprecedented scale.

Today nothing much has changed. Agribusiness corporations still claim their methods to be science-led. By implication those who believe ecological farming systems to be a safer and more secure way to feed the world are driven by some anti-science agenda.

If you read the farming press these days you'd think corporate agriculture was the only game in town. Taking its lead from the scientists at Rothamsted, the Syngenta corporation – turnover nearly £9 billion – announced a plan to increase global crop yields in seven years.[10] Science-driven farming, delivered in partnership with farmers on the ground, was the sustainable solution to the world's food security and environmental problems, said the company.

Not to be outdone, the chemical company BASF took a full-page ad in the farming press and toadied up its farmer customers with the accolade: 'Farming, the biggest job on earth.'[11] The ad went on: 'In less than forty years there will be three billion more people on the planet. So growing enough food of the right quality, from the land available, is going to be an increasingly tough task. This is why BASF is working with farmers to create chemistry which is helping to maximise yields and produce fitter, healthier crops.'

In *Opportunity Agriculture*, a report produced for the 2014 Oxford Farming Conference, the authors lash out at the 'Luddite attitudes' that have left Europe free of GM crops.[12] New biological knowledge – cis-genetics and synthetic biology – must not be allowed to fall into the same trap. The cost of doing so would be 'catastrophic'. Food production would fail to meet the food needs of the world's growing population. The report was sponsored by Syngenta.

At the same conference – a year earlier – environmentalist Mark Lynas had caused a minor sensation when he apologised for having ripped up GM crops in the mid-1990s, so helping to start the anti-GM movement. He went on to condemn the movement as 'immoral and inhumane' given the challenges the world faced in feeding its population and preserving the environment. Lynas attributed his damascene conversion to his having 'discovered science'.

Perhaps spurred on by Lynas's saint-like confession of past sins, Britain's former Environment Secretary Owen Paterson condemned environmental groups who opposed GM crops in Africa and Asia as 'absolutely wicked'. The particular bit of genome wizardry he was defending was 'golden rice', a genetically-altered variety said to raise the level of vitamin A precursor in the diets of undernourished people. At the time the rice hadn't been assessed as safe in any country, and there remained doubts about whether it would work.

This didn't deter the Environment Secretary in his determination to root out wickedness. It was, he ranted, 'just disgusting that little children are allowed to go blind and die because of a hang-up by a small number of people about this technology'. His outburst won the backing of *The Times*. In a leader it thundered: 'GM crops are no more unnatural than the millennia-old practices of raising conventional crops or domesticating animals. They make human beings at home in the world and advance the welfare of the poorest people on Earth.'

All this after several hundred of the world's leading agricultural scientists had decided that natural biological systems were likely to make a better job of feeding us all than the laboratory creations of plant science and the persuasive powers of rich corporations. I wondered how Professor Hans Herren, chief author of the long-ignored World Bank study, felt about the orchestrated undermining of his ground-breaking report. I got the chance to ask him when he travelled from his home in the US to address an all-party group in the House of Commons.

Professor Herren knows a thing or two about feeding poor people. For many years he worked in Africa researching sustainable, ecologically-based farming systems. As director of a major research centre in Benin he conceived and implemented a biological pest control programme that saved the African cassava crop and averted the continent's worst-ever food crisis. In 1995 he was awarded the World Food Prize, given to individuals who improve the quality or availability of food.

So how did he feel about the sidelining of his report, I asked him as we sat in a coffee shop just off Parliament Square. He seemed remarkably chipper in the circumstances. If he viewed this as a setback he wasn't showing it. His position remained uncompromising.

The present food system had clearly failed, he said. It had caused a billion people to go hungry and stay poor, while another billion, in rich countries, had been made overweight or obese. It had also ruined topsoil, reduced biodiversity, damaged the environment, robbed rural communities of their livelihoods and transferred the costs of all these to the public.

Hardly a catalogue of achievement. When things had gone so terribly wrong there was only one rational response – to reinvent agriculture along more ecological lines. He laid the responsibility for all this on his fellow scientists. Agricultural research needed to head in a new direction. It needed to focus on small-scale farmers with an emphasis on the role of women. It was the kind of research that could only be funded by the public sector.

So where did that leave the global corporations who are currently driving farming policy in the industrial west? According to Herren, it would be better for the world if they simply left the stage. 'Despite the scare stories there's a need to de-intensify agriculture in Europe and other developed countries', he told me. 'We're actually over-producing food in the world. In energy terms it's about twice what we need to keep people healthy. The real problem is we're growing it in the wrong places by the wrong methods.

'In the developed countries we need to grow less food of higher quality using fewer chemical inputs. In developing countries where the food is needed we could easily double production using organic or ecological methods. I know this is possible because I've done the research myself.'

Herren's formula for European agriculture reads like a manifesto for the traditional mixed farm. He wants farms that produce a wide range of nutrient-rich foods and employ skilled people. Just as the mixed farm did. He wants farms that maintain biodiversity and protect watercourses from pollution. The mixed farm is perfect for protecting the countryside. And he wants shorter supply lines between farm and retailer, with shops stocking many more local foods.

Before the state took over agriculture, Britain's towns and cities were surrounded by small mixed farms supplying local shops. They didn't need subsidies to survive. In fact, subsidies were their undoing. It's large industrial farms and the companies supplying them that have grown rich on taxpayers' money.

What's interesting about Herren's wish-list is that he hasn't proposed it for the benefit of Britain, though it clearly would be. It's part of a new paradigm for feeding the world, better and more sustainably. Here's a world expert – backed by others across the world – who says that modern, industrial agriculture is not the solution to world food problems. It's the principal cause of them.

It's a view you seldom hear in Britain these days. Instead,

the unhealthy alliance of public science and big-business agriculture keeps up the fiction that without their gene tinkering and chemicals the world goes to hell in a handcart. It's a simple message of self-interest. In a truly sustainable farming system of the sort proposed by Professor Herren, sales of chemical fertilisers and pesticides would dwindle away as soils became more fertile. The one thing the agribusiness corporations can be guaranteed not to do is choke off their own sales.

By getting into bed with them, the government is effectively blocking any advance to real sustainability. Rather they are backing the agribusiness interpretation of the word, one that would make UK agriculture forever dependent on chemicals and hybrid seeds – and probably GM crops. When the Crop Protection Association (CPA) – trade body for the pesticide manufacturers – warns that rising world populations threaten higher food prices, it's really about protecting sales.

'Access to the latest advances in plant science – in crop genetics, agro-chemistry and agronomy – will be needed to help keep the lid on food price inflation by ensuring food supplies keep pace with the demands of population growth', the CPA's boss Dominic Dyer told a Glasgow meeting of teachers and health professionals.[13] What the teachers won't hear is that there's a far more effective way of feeding the world and keeping food prices down. We could increase production in developing countries and switch to genuinely sustainable, chemical-free farming at home.

Backed by the big-spending biotech companies, the Foresight report got the media exposure that was denied to the earlier World Bank report. The alliance of big science and big business won over the policy-makers and ultimately the Treasury. Herren's vision of the world's poorest countries feeding themselves rather than being reliant on the technology of companies like Monsanto and Syngenta has been removed from the food debate.

The UK government dutifully came up with its new £160 million research package. This so-called 'agri-tech strategy' will support 'agricultural innovation' by promoting collaboration and co-investment from industry. Since industry is solely interested in developing new products, this is where most of the cash will go.

The winners are the plant scientists who spend their lives trying out new gene combinations in the lab, and also the biotech companies whose ambition is to earn royalties on every seed sold to farmers. The losers will be the many farmers who would dearly love to produce healthier foods by genuinely sustainable methods. And, of course, everyone else on these islands; all of us who eat food. In fact, the whole world.

Britain's wheat growers are obsessed with new technology. The pages of the farming press are full of stories about the latest gadgets and gizmos that will supposedly make them more efficient. We're not just talking about the new chemicals and gene combinations flowing from the grand alliance of biotech companies and public research centres.

Small and intermediate companies are queuing up to sell farmers driverless tractors, global positioning systems, drones, data-handling equipment and 'isobus', the connectivity standard that allows tractors to talk to other implements such as crop-sprayers and seed drills.

To pay for all this technology, farmers have to drive their land harder; to extract yet more grain from their overworked soils. Alternatively they can strive to get bigger by buying up more land, so spreading their overheads across more hectares. This is one of the reasons why, in the decade up to 2013, UK farmland prices rose at a faster rate than even prime central London residential property.

Modern wheat growing is less about feeding people than making profits for private companies, large and small. The latest buzz-phrase beloved of both politicians and agribusiness executives is making British agriculture 'sustainably competitive'. This is shorthand for driving down the cost per tonne of grain so it can compete on world markets. But what it amounts to is a race to the bottom, a global contest to wreck soils and rob foods of nutrients.

At a Westminster seminar on 'Implementing the UK Strategy for Agricultural Technologies', one of the speakers, Clare Bend, was queried over a diagram she showed during her talk. Clare Bend is head of technology at Agrii, a company that provides professional agronomists and products for arable farmers. As we've heard, agronomists are the people who advise farmers what sprays and fertilisers to put on next.

At the seminar, Bend was asked why her diagram on crop pests and disease appeared to show no benefits from improving soil fertility. The questioner from the audience held up a copy of a book by Sir Albert Howard, a plant scientist of the mid-20th century. 'Was the speaker aware', the questioner asked, 'that Howard, an adviser to both the British and Indian governments, had achieved remarkable reductions in crop pests and diseases simply by improving the soil?'

Though the Westminster seminar included some of today's leading crop scientists, both from the public sector and industry, it's unlikely that any of them would have been familiar with Howard's writings. But with many of Britain's soils on the edge of collapse, his work is of immediate value to today's farmers, unlike the as-yet empty promises of largely untested technologies including GM crops.

Howard, who spent much of his research career in India, established clear links between crop health and human vitality. He became convinced that fertile soils – rich in humus from the breakdown of plant and animal wastes – were essential for growing healthy foods. He wrote that crop plants were nourished in two ways.[14] First they absorbed through their roots small quantities of nitrate, phosphate and potash salts from solution in soil. But they also relied on the symbiotic relationship with mycorrhizal fungi – thread-like soil fungi – for many other nutrients.

Only when plants were nourished in this dual way were they able to take up all the trace elements they needed. And only then could they resist disease and produce high-quality foods for both animals and human beings, wrote Howard.

In marked contrast, crops grown with chemical fertilisers were only partially nourished. Chemical farming destroyed soil humus and severed the link between crop roots and mycorrhizal fungi. This meant crops were no longer able to withstand disease attack. Nor were they able to protect human health as well as foods produced from well-nourished crops.

Much of Howard's work was done more than 80 years ago. To today's plant scientists immersed in gene technology and molecular biology it's of little interest, except perhaps as a historical curiosity. But in the United States a soil microbiologist – whose name is fast becoming known around the world – has endorsed Howard's views.

Through her work in the Forest Soils department of Oregon State University, Dr Elaine Ingham has begun to shed light on the complex subterranean world of soil microbes. Together they make up an interdependent web of microscopic life, which includes bacteria, fungi, protozoa, nematodes and small arthropods. This is what she has termed the Soil Food Web.[15]

To Ingham it's this hidden world that allows our planet and society to function. She's convinced that it's as crucial for our health as breathing. Yet modern farming, far from nurturing this web of life on which we depend, often destroys it. Each time the soil is disturbed – or chemical fertilisers and pesticides are applied – soil organisms are killed and soil structure damaged.

This is why our soils are eroding. It's also why farmers are having to spend thousands of pounds on chemical sprays and artificial fertilisers. Their soils are dysfunctional. Without the chemicals they can grow nothing. But if the microbial life in their soils were flourishing they wouldn't need the chemicals.[16]

All this is lost on today's cereal growers, so ingrained is

the chemical habit. Most are convinced that it's technology, not a healthy soil, that will secure their future, even though making a profit becomes daily more difficult.

If you want an idea of the stranglehold the biotech giants currently exert on arable farmers, it's worth going along to the annual Cereals Event, a crop technology jamboree that takes place each year in early summer. The one I visited was held on a broad, open plateau in the heart of Britain's wheat-growing country in Lincolnshire. From the parking area I walked towards a small city of marquees, trade stands, machinery lines and crop demonstration plots. With its fluttering flags and banners the whole scene looked like a medieval army on the move.

I strolled among the crowded trade stands. The year's crop of new farm machines looked bigger than ever. There were giant combine harvesters capable of devouring many hectares of wheat in a single day. Ranks of heavy-duty cultivators stood ready to stir up and shatter the soil in readiness for the next crop.

New wheat varieties were much in evidence. Biotech companies are constantly introducing new hybrids that promise a little more yield or slightly improved disease resistance. But the real stars of this Big Wheat Fest were chemicals – the fertilisers and pesticides that underpin crop growing across the western world. And the largest, plushest trade stands belonged to the companies that market them.

These are the warlords of this occupation army, the powers that keep industrial wheat growing the dominant force across a big slice of Britain. And everywhere at this great rural trade show their justification was science. The signs on the company stands proclaimed it loud and clear. 'Led by science', said one banner. 'The product of science', said another. No visitor to this show could have failed to understand that this system of food growing was the product of cold, rational, scientific thought.

I thought of the great 20th-century agricultural scientist George Stapledon. Towards the end of his career he became disillusioned with science, which he believed was taking agriculture in a dangerous direction. He was alarmed by increasing specialisation in farming, particularly the emergence of crop monocultures across large areas of Britain. He became highly critical of his fellow agricultural scientists for focusing too narrowly on new technologies. He believed this approach was fraught with risk.

After more than 40 years in research, Stapledon had become convinced that each new attempt to control nature was likely to lead to unforeseen dangers. How could it be otherwise when natural systems were so complex? No experiment could be devised to unravel the full impact of any new technology. That's why he believed that great caution should be exercised before ancient knowledge was discarded in favour of new technology. And he didn't see much caution being exercised by his fellow agricultural scientists.

'In putting all our money on narrow specialisation and on the newly dawned age of technology, we have backed a wild horse which, given its head, is bound to get out of control', Stapledon wrote to fellow scientists in 1956.[17]

I was reminded of Stapledon's warning when, at a

conference on plant science, I heard a leading molecular biologist remark that GM technology was so safe it hardly needed regulating. When a leading scientist loses proper objectivity you know you're going to be in trouble.

A few years later the American public interest attorney Steven Druker was to write in his book on the development of GM technology that 'the myriad distortions, deceptions and downright lies issued by scientists and scientific institutions … constitute the most colossal and pernicious scientific fraud ever perpetrated; and besides the serious damage they've done to the integrity of science, they've imposed unacceptable risks on human and environmental health.'[18]

In modern Britain our fascination with technology knows no bounds. Nor does our reverence for science and scientists. Politicians who declare they're being led by the science have a perfect get-out clause whatever the outcome of their decisions. Unfortunately for the rest of us, science often comes up with the wrong answer, or at best a partial answer. In the 1990s the scientific consensus was that the BSE prion wouldn't jump the species barrier, so we were all safe from mad cow disease. Years later the scientists decided it could after all. We were all left worrying about how many cheap burgers we'd eaten a couple of decades earlier.

We kid ourselves that science is objective. In our rational, post-Enlightenment age we're ready to drop knowledge systems that are thousands of years old. Farmers have known for centuries how to grow healthy foods in sustainable ways.

But unless there's been a peer-reviewed research paper on it in the past twenty years it doesn't count for anything. Which might be fine if the scientists could be relied upon to look at the things that matter. But they don't. They look at what they're paid to look at.

'Golden rice', the GM variety supposed to improve vitamin A nutrition in poor countries, has received millions of dollars in development funding. Compare this with the naturally occurring soil fungi known as arbuscular mycorrhizal fungi, which have been known for centuries to increase the uptake of trace elements by plants. Research funding for this vital process has been virtually non-existent, mainly because large corporations have so far seen no way of privatising it for shareholder profit.

I used to know an ex-farmer who'd spent 30 years investigating the role of mycorrhizae in promoting the uptake of minerals by crop plants. John Reeves had become very knowledgeable about the role of mineral elements in the health of both humans and animals. You might think such an important topic was best suited to publicly-funded research. Unfortunately a great deal of our research money is spent on the development of new technologies for private companies.

All too often it's left to dedicated amateurs like John Reeves to carry out the studies that matter. No one paid him for the work. He felt compelled to do it following a period farming on Vancouver Island in Canada, when a trace element deficiency caused widespread sickness in his sheep flock.

In his studies Reeves had the support of a university scientist who carried out the trace element analyses of crop samples, and another at Rothamsted research station. Otherwise alone and unsupported, the amateur scientist found out that soils with healthy populations of mycorrhizae produced crops and vegetables with two-thirds more health-promoting trace elements than those grown on soils fertilised with chemicals.[19]

To my knowledge no professional scientist in either the public sector or the corporate world has taken up this great work. Retired farmers like Reeves don't have the clout of the Monsantos of this world.

One of my favourite books on farming is by the Japanese farmer Masanobu Fukuoka. It's called, intriguingly, *The One-Straw Revolution*. In it the author, himself a trained microbiologist, explains how he developed a system for growing rice without any of the chemical fertilisers and pesticides that mainstream farmers rely on. Even so he produced crops that were as good as any in all Japan.

According to Fukuoka, the reason modern chemicals appear necessary for food production is that the natural balance has been so badly disturbed by these methods, the land has become dependent on them. Nature, left alone, is in perfect balance, he wrote. Harmful insects and plant diseases are always present, but don't reach damaging levels. The sensible approach to disease and pest control is to grow sturdy crops in a healthy environment.

In developing his system Fukuoka carried out his own experiments in growing crops, always with the idea of developing a method close to nature. Modern scientific agriculture has no such vision, he says. Instead research wanders about aimlessly, each researcher seeing just one part of the infinite array of natural factors that affect harvest yields.

Nature is divided into small pieces. The tests then carried out conform neither with natural law nor with practical experience. To think that these conclusions can be put to use with invariable success in the farmer's field is a big mistake.

We have allowed a small cabal of laboratory scientists and their corporate backers to change the very nature of the food we eat. They have substituted their own technologies for the natural processes that have fed humankind since we evolved on the planet. And they are fast destroying the land that feeds us.

No one asked us if we wanted our food produced by Monsanto and Syngenta rather than by nature. There's been no national debate; no referendum, though it would be hard to think of an issue more important than the nature of our food. The silent revolution has been mostly brought about by the secretive lobbying of governments and public servants.

Fortunately we now have the knowledge and means to reverse the takeover of our food supply. It's an opportunity presented to us by our grasslands. All we have to do, each one of us, is insist that the meat and dairy foods we eat come from animals grazing pasture. It will mean our diets are healthier. Even more important, we'll be putting nature back in charge of our food supply. When that happens we can sleep a lot easier.

CHAPTER 6

The power of pasture

From a hilltop near my home in west Somerset you can see the nation's energy future – or part of it. It's a cluster of geometric blocks that make up the nuclear power station at Hinkley Point. From a distance it looks like an oversized Turner Prize entry that's been dumped on the shores of the Bristol Channel.

Here atoms are split to send power crackling through the wires across the flat Somerset countryside. Electricity to heat our kettles and light up our flat-screen TVs. We marvel at the technology and grumble at the extra charges on our energy bills. And we try not to think too much about the nuclear catastrophe at Fukushima.

You can see our energy past from this hilltop too. It's scrawled on the chequer-board field pattern stretching down to the water's edge. There's another form of energy transformation going on here. It's so familiar that we hardly notice it any more. Yet it has the power to make us healthier and to slash the cost of the NHS. It would give the economy its biggest boost since North Sea oil. It might even allow us to beat our carbon emission targets. Not bad for a technology that's virtually free.

Alongside our house there's a little field so steep that the locals used to call it 'the cliff'. Visitors to the village gaze up in amazement that our small flock of Exmoor sheep manage to stay on their feet to graze. For as long as anyone can remember no one's been suicidal enough to venture on it with a tractor. So unlike most of Britain's grasslands it has never been sprayed with weedkiller or spread with chemical fertilisers. The ancient turf still contains the sorts of grasses and wildflowers you don't see on the ruthlessly efficient farms of today. It's what the naturalists call 'unimproved acid grassland'.

Key players in the rich mix of species are a dozen or so different grasses of the kind modern agriculture would consider 'unproductive'. Their names are as rich as our rural past: meadow foxtail, cocksfoot, sweet vernal grass, Yorkshire fog and crested dog's-tail. Then there are the wild clovers. You can find both the red- and white-flowering types on our ancient turf.

From June onwards it's studded with a succession of wild flowering plants and herbs. They include meadow vetchling, yarrow, sheep's sorrel, buttercup, salad burnet, plantain, burnet saxifrage, lady's bedstraw, rough hawkbit and the yellow-and-orange nitrogen-fixing plant, bird's-foot trefoil, known in my part of Somerset as eggs-and-bacon.

Modern, business-minded farmers wouldn't give a 'thank you' for pastures like this. They would consider them hopelessly uneconomic, fit only for some nature reserve where production is unimportant. In their place, profit-oriented farmers would plant single-species 'monocultures' selected from a small number of fast-growing grasses to which they apply large amounts of chemical fertiliser. But in doing so they may be making a big mistake.

Our own small sheep flock seem to thrive on our old-fashioned, flower-filled grassland. Though they've now reached an advanced age (for sheep) they remain healthy and strong, staying out in all weathers, winter and summer. We spend nothing on the wormers and medicines that fill the veterinary cupboards of most commercial sheep farms. The herbs in the pasture seem to take care of most ailments. On their salad-bar diets they grow thick wool fleeces of high quality, as well as rearing a lamb or two with no extra feeding.

There's a reason why sheep do well on this ancient grassland. They're nourished and protected by a teeming population of living organisms in the soil beneath them. There are billions in every cubic centimetre: bacteria, fungi and single-celled protozoa such as amoebae. Higher up the food chain there are worm-like nematodes as well as arthropods, small animals such as beetles with segmented limbs and hard exoskeletons made of a substance called chitin.

Unlikely as it may seem, it's the interplay of this seething mass of underground life that determines whether the food we eat will protect our health or lead to malnutrition and sickness. Together they produce the nutrients to feed crop plants and the defences to protect them from disease. They also open up the network of underground airways and passages through which roots can grow. In control of the whole extraordinary process are plants. They provide the energy that most underground life-forms need to function. In doing so they drive a process that's millions of years old, and which functions most efficiently in old, species-rich grassland like mine.

Through the process of photosynthesis, plants use the energy of sunlight to bond carbon atoms together and make sugars. While some of these are used by the plant for its own growth, many are passed through the roots to feed soil microbes. These sweet hand-outs are known as root 'exudates'. Plants use them to attract the kinds of bacteria and fungi they need to their roots.

The exact composition of the exudates will vary depending on the plant's requirements at any particular time. It may put out the kind of sweetener that will attract bacteria and fungi to defend its roots against disease attack. At another time the exudates will attract the kinds of bacteria that will supply an essential nutrient element such as zinc.

Key intermediaries in the relationship between plants and soil microbes are the group of thread-like fungi known as arbuscular mycorrhizal fungi. These free-living soil organisms grow as tiny filaments, 1/25th the diameter of a human hair. They form intimate links (known as mycorrhizae) with plant roots, actually penetrating the cells of the root cortex. It's a mutually beneficial arrangement known in biology as symbiosis. The plant supplies the fungus with carbohydrates and amino acids in its sap. In return the fungus supplies the plant with minerals, helps it to withstand drought and protects it against harmful disease organisms in the soil.

In effect, mycorrhizae form an extension of the plant's root system. They dramatically increase the surface area across which the plant can trade nutrients for soil minerals such as phosphorus, zinc, copper and magnesium. Amazingly, they can increase the plant's uptake of these essential minerals up to 60 times. Mycorrhizae are also the main route through which plants pass exudates – their 'sweeteners' – to other soil microbes. Mycorrhizal fungi are the plant's partners in gathering the right sort of microbes around its roots so it can stay well-nourished and healthy.

This is why these little-known organisms are essential to plant health and ultimately to human health. Without them, plants – including crop plants – cannot take up the nutrients they need. In old, species-rich pastures like mine they thrive, forming links with many of the turf grasses and herbs. But the methods of mainstream farming damage or destroy them. The chemical fertilisers, pesticides and intensive cultivations used by most farmers harm them or kill them off altogether. And this harms us.

Because they're plugged into this extraordinary underground ecosystem, old grasslands like mine require no chemical fertilizers or pesticides to stay productive. The plants themselves – both grasses and herbs – put out foods to grow the billions of bacteria needed to supply them with essential nutrients. And they grow the miles of fungal filament required to feed them and protect them from disease attack.

So long as there's sunlight and rain the process continues. It never runs down. It doesn't slow up from exhaustion. The plants keep on growing, their leaves packed with nutrients. These are eaten by grazing animals – like my own little flock of Exmoor sheep. They, too, are part of the process. They chomp the leaves, taking in the nutrients they need to stay healthy.

As we've seen, grazing animals like cattle and sheep are ruminants. They don't directly digest the vegetation that makes up the bulk of their diets. Instead the food is passed into the rumen, a large fermentation chamber where the material is broken down by the action of microbes. Most of the soluble nutrients are released this way, though unfermented fibre – together with some other materials – passes through to the lower gastrointestinal tract for digestion by enzymes.

Since so much of the ruminant diet is made up of cellulose, it seems odd that ruminant animals haven't evolved enzymes capable of breaking it down, relying instead on microbes in the rumen. Cellulose is a polysaccharide, a compound constructed chiefly of glucose units linked together by a special chemical bond. Cellulase, the enzyme capable of breaking this bond, is produced by a number of bacteria, fungi and seedlings, but not by animals.

Cellulose is a structural polysaccharide found in plant cell walls. It's one of the most abundant of all compounds found in living organisms. So it's something of a conundrum that animals living mainly on vegetation don't have the means of digesting it directly. American agronomist and grazier Bill Murphy thinks the lifestyle of grazing animals may have been the reason for the development of the rumen.

With few defences against predators, grazers would probably have left the protection of the forest for as little time as possible. They'd have quickly eaten their fill of plants growing in exposed clearings of the forest or at the forest edge, then retired to the safety of the trees to digest the food.

Instead of producing cellulase to digest the food

immediately, they came to rely on vast numbers of symbiotic micro-organisms living in the digestive tract. These break down fibrous and soluble plant material by fermentation, effectively becoming the animal's cellulase-producing tissue. It's a slow process, but one well suited to an animal that spends a minimal amount of time gathering food and long periods lying quietly in hidden places.[1]

Ruminants use grass by first swallowing it, then later regurgitating the coarser material as cud. In a safe place the animal chews it a second time before swallowing it back into the rumen. There volatile organic acids such as acetic, propionic and butyric acids – produced by rumen micro-organisms – become the animal's main energy sources. Micro-organisms also supply amino acids – the essential building blocks for proteins – together with vitamin K and B vitamins.

Ruminants extract many more healthy nutrients from mixed-species pastures like my patch of old grassland than from commercial grass 'monocultures'. When we eat their meat we get the benefits too. Plants that are well nourished by the microbial life of the soil produce a vast range of chemical compounds. They include enzymes, hormones, sterols, carbohydrates, fats and many thousands of substances known as phytochemicals.

Plants produce these compounds for their own purposes, of course, but through evolution grazing animals – and humans – have come to rely on them for their protection, too. Among the many compounds produced in plant 'factories' are pigments such as carotenoids, zeaxanthin and resveratrol, all powerful antioxidants. Plants need them for protection against UV radiation, diseases, insect pests and even against premature 'ageing', known in plants as senescence. Together these pigments are part of the plant's 'immune system'.

When animals and humans eat the plants they accumulate these pigments in their fat, boosting their own immune systems. They reduce inflammation, neutralise damaging free-radicals and help moderate hormone systems. Pasture plants are also important sources of omega-3 fatty acids. As we've seen, the meat and milk of animals grazing on pastures are rich in these essential fats that are vital to human health. Among their chief metabolic functions are helping in the normal development of the foetus and fighting heart disease.

Ruminant animals grazing have another great gift for humans. In their rumens they synthesise the amazing substance CLA, conjugated linoleic acid, one of the most powerful cancer-fighters known in nature. Grazing pastures and the fertile, living soils that support them are part of the incredible ecosystem that protects our health. But in using our present food and farming methods we seem to be doing our level best to destroy it.

Plant roots feed microbes. The microbes feed the plant. The plant feeds grazing animals. The whole cycle is powered by the energy of the sun. It's a process that's millions of years old. There's fossil evidence to suggest that the fungus–root relationship played a key role in the colonisation of land by plants. It's also clear that the earliest human beings ate animal foods produced in this way. On this land we now call Britain, studies show that early humans were killing and eating the meat of grazing animals more than 400,000 years ago.[2]

For most of this time humans and their ancestors took the foods they wanted from the natural system they were part of. But the hunter evolved into the farmer. Humans were no longer content to collect a harvest from their environment. They wanted to control it. They began herding the animals they'd bred across the grasslands they'd cleared of forest.

They learned when to graze an area of pasture and when to move the animals on to the next. They learned how long an interval to leave the pasture before returning to graze it once more. Through trial and error they learned the secret of fertility – how to increase it and how easily it could be squandered.

Today the pasture field is the arena in which grasses and humans enact their ritual encounters so both can thrive. In the process of photosynthesis the leaves of pasture plants capture sunlight, using the energy to convert carbon dioxide and water into simple sugars. More than 90 per cent of a plant's dry weight is made up of organic compounds derived from these simple sugars.

Green leaves – like all living tissues – also respire; they burn sugars to produce the energy they need for metabolism, releasing carbon dioxide and water in the process. In effect it's photosynthesis in reverse. In bright sunlight the amount of carbon converted into sugars is far higher than the carbon lost in respiration. So the pasture becomes more dense.

But at low light levels the rate of photosynthesis falls. As the growing grass gets thicker, more leaves are shaded by those above them. Eventually a point is reached when more sugars are being burned by respiration than are being formed by photosynthesis. When this happens the older leaves start to die back and much of the production is wasted.

The farmer's job is to move animals onto a pasture – or a part of the pasture – while it's still growing and adding vegetation. The trick is to move them to the next pasture area before they've grazed too close to the ground. If this happens there won't be enough leaf tissue left for the grass to recover quickly. The plants will have to draw upon carbohydrate reserves in the roots, a process that can delay recovery by several days.

At the start of the growing season – or following a spell of grazing – pastures follow an S-shaped sigmoid pattern of growth. Early on there's a period of slow but accelerating growth. Then there's a period of rapid growth, followed by a spell of slow and declining growth. Knowing how to manage this recurring pattern of growth and regrowth is the art of good grazing.

It's an art that has been the gateway to health and prosperity for generations of country people. For centuries, village communities in the wild uplands of the north and west of Britain followed the custom of taking their cattle up to the 'shielings' – mountain grazings – during the summer months. The shieling system – part of a livestock-herding culture dating back to Neolithic times – was widely practised in high country right across Europe, still surviving today in parts of Norway, Sweden and the Alps.[3]

The seasonal use of mountain pastures meant that more cattle could be kept than the main holding alone would support. Each year part of the village community – often the girls and young women – would live in rudimentary huts high in the hills, close to the upland grazings. There they would pass the summer months milking the cows and making the butter and cheese that would help sustain their families through the winter.

In the autumn the animals would be returned to the village where they would spend the winter on the lowland pastures, or be fed on hay and root crops such as turnips and swedes. Surplus animals could be slaughtered and their meat salted down, or handed over to drovers for sale in the markets of the south and east.

The presence of grazing animals trampling and dunging on the turf during the summer gradually improved the pasture, making it more productive year by year. The young women herders were skilled at knowing exactly when to move their cattle off one stretch of grass and on to the next. As a result they were able to produce large amounts of food from terrain that today would be considered harsh and unproductive.

There are good grounds for thinking that the meat and milk produced on the shielings were rich in vitamins and protective fats. Certainly the villagers themselves were convinced that the butter they made on the summer pastures was better-tasting and healthier than any produced on the lowlands.

The next breakthrough in the art of grazing came from an unlikely source. Edinburgh-born James Anderson is best remembered for his theory of ground rent, an idea taken up by the English economist David Ricardo. But in a text dated 1791 Anderson also gives a full and lucid account of what's now known as rotational grazing – the practice of grazing a small area of pasture in a paddock, then moving the animals on quickly to the next paddock.

It's a way of increasing the intensity of grazing and increasing the output of meat and milk from a given area of pasture. Today a small but growing number of farmers are reviving it using electric fencing to turn their grass fields into a number of small paddocks. Most would be surprised to learn that the technique's more than two centuries old.

Anderson wrote: 'Instead of allowing his beasts to roam indiscriminately through the whole area at once, he [the farmer] collects the whole number of beasts that he intends to feed into one flock, and turns them all at once into one of these divisions; which, being quite fresh, and of sufficient length for a full bite, would please their palate so much as to induce them to eat it greedily, and fill their bellies before they thought of roaming about, and thus destroying it with their feet.

'If there were just so many parks [divisions] as there required days to make the grass of these fields advance to a proper length after being eaten bare down, the first field would be ready to receive them by the time they had gone over all the others; so that they might thus be carried round in a constant rotation.'[4]

There's no record of how many farmers adopted the technique in the late 18th century. But two centuries later a French biochemist called André Voisin showed how it could produce large amounts of food without ruining the land. Voisin taught biochemistry at the French National Veterinary School. He was a laureate member of France's Academy of Agriculture, and held an honorary doctorate from Bonn University. But at heart he was a farmer, running a small farm near Dieppe that had been in the family for generations.

In the 1950s Voisin carried out a series of grazing studies to investigate the productivity of pastures. He developed a technique he called 'rational grazing' in which cattle were moved around a succession of small paddocks rather than being allowed to graze over a whole field. He made the remarkable discovery that pastures grazed in this ordered way produced more food per hectare than arable crops.

It was an extraordinary finding. Had it been acted upon by our own government and the farming establishment it might well have given Britain a healthy and sustainable food supply. The chances are there'd have been no BSE scare, and the fields and streams of this green and pleasant land would have been cleaner and less polluted.

Voisin's discovery was that – to be productive – pastures needed regular rest periods, rather like workers in a factory. His inspiration was a classic time-and-motion study carried out by Frederick Winslow Taylor for the Bethlehem Steel Company in 1890s America. The study involved a team of men whose job it was to carry ingots of high-carbon pig-iron. It was hard physical toil, and Taylor tried to measure the amount of work the staff could do before becoming fatigued.

To his surprise he found that the level of fatigue didn't depend on the weight of iron carried. The least tired workers were those who carried their ingots or 'pigs' fastest. This allowed them to take longer returning for the next pig without attracting the attention of the foreman. Taylor observed that when workers were given sufficient rest, they could shift three times more iron than before.

Voisin applied the same principle to the management of grassland. No one had ever considered the needs of the plants before. By dividing up grass fields with fences, he was able to rotate the herd of grazing cattle around the various paddocks, giving the grass in each paddock a chance to recuperate before the cattle came back again. When pastures were allowed this rest period they produced three times more vegetation over the season than when livestock were able to range over them at will.

When Voisin published his findings in a book called *Grass Productivity* (1957), they caused much excitement in the world of farming. Here was an opportunity to boost food output without incurring great expense for the farmer. For a nation like Britain desperate to secure more home-grown food, the new findings held great promise.

British scientists took up the theme. William Davies, former director of the Grassland Research Institute, urged the widespread adoption of mixed farming in which arable land was regularly sown with a grass crop to increase its fertility. He warned that land maintained under a monoculture of cereals often ended up in poor shape, particularly after a drought.

There was also the risk of soil erosion when land was cropped with cereals for too long. In phrases that seem even more relevant today, Davies wrote: 'If the world is to feed itself better – and at the same time increase its population – it must farm its soils better than it has ever done in the past. It has become increasingly apparent that the grass crop plays a more fundamental role than any other.'[5]

For a few years grass farming boomed. Hundreds of farmers made the trip to Normandy to look at André Voisin's famous grazing pastures. By the 1960s the enthusiasm for grasslands and the foods they produced was at its height. Among the enthusiasts was Somerset farmer Frank Newman Turner, author of a popular book called *Fertility Farming*. Turner was against the popular practice of sowing new pastures with just one or two modern grass varieties. He believed farm pastures should be like wild or semi-natural pastures, containing a variety of deep-rooting herb species as well as grasses.

His own sown grasslands included 30 or more different plant species, including up to nine varieties of agricultural grass, four types of clover, and a variety of herb species such as chicory, burnet, yarrow, sheep's parsley, kidney vetch, lucerne and plantain. Even dandelion seeds found their way into the mix.[6]

In the book telling the story of Goosegreen, his farm near Bridgwater, Turner wrote that seed mixtures like this were essential if the land were to stay fertile and grazing animals were to be properly nourished. A pasture with deep-rooting herbs aerated the soil and helped collect essential minerals and trace elements from deep down in the subsoil. Especially important were herbs like chicory, burnet, lucerne and dandelion, all of which penetrated to a depth of a metre or more.

Turner shunned chemical fertilisers and pesticides. Having relied on them early in his farming career he became convinced they were damaging to his animals and crops, and ruinous of his land. He came to depend instead on organic compost and herb-rich pastures for the fertility that would give him good wheat crops and healthy cattle. It seems they worked remarkably well.

He believed that by providing his cattle with diverse, mineral-rich pasture he was able to prevent – and even cure – many of the most crippling animal diseases, including bovine tuberculosis, infertility, mastitis and Johnes disease, an inflammatory condition of the gut similar to Crohn's disease in humans, and thought to be caused by para-tuberculosis bacteria in milk. All these diseases are common in Britain's cattle population today.

What made these pasture-based food systems so productive – and sustainable – is that they were based on natural processes millions of years old. Natural grasslands are never made up of a single species. They can contain dozens of species of grass, clovers and herbs. The precise mix of species in the grassland 'community', as it's called, depends on such factors as the soil type, the nature of the underlying rock, height above sea level, topography and climate. Each is unique to its location.

The mix of species is never static. As environmental conditions change, so some species become more numerous at the expense of others. For example, a period of drought will result in the decline of some species, while others – such as deep-rooting, drought-resistant grasses and herbs – will strengthen their hold on the pasture community. The whole ecology of the pasture is in a constant state of flux.

When grazing animals spread their dung across a pasture they raise the fertility of the underlying soil. This encourages the more productive, faster-growing grass species at the expense of slow-growing grasses. As the productive species gradually become dominant in the pasture, the nutrition of the grazing animal improves. This means it excretes droppings that are more nutrient-rich, and this in turn ratchets up the fertility cycle of the soil.

So, properly managed, the whole grazing system becomes more and more productive. Without any artificial chemical inputs, the food output of the land increases. So does the nutritional value of this food. André Voisin described it as an 'organic spiral of production', which progressively enriches the soil and brings about a steady increase in the production of well-managed pastures.[7]

Today the art of grazing has been largely lost. Few farmers believe grassland alone can produce much food, and certainly not without massive applications of chemical nitrate fertiliser. For the most part, livestock farmers prefer to feed their animals on grains and industrial crops like maize. However costly and inefficient this kind of farming may be, it is at least predictable and measurable. For a given amount of feed energy put in you can, up to a point, predict the output of meat and milk you'll get in return.

But, as we'll find out, a few pioneering American graziers are proving not merely that pastures can be productive, but that they are the only environmentally-friendly way of producing large amounts of food. Likewise in Britain, a group of 'free-range' milk producers are discovering that the young women who ran their cattle on the summer shielings knew a thing or two about producing healthy foods.

A new generation of graziers has found that by mimicking the grazing cycles of the great natural grasslands, they can produce large amounts of beef and milk at low cost and in ways that benefit the environment. And, as we've seen, the foods from grass are invariably healthy.

In a small way my own little sheep flock shows just how productive mixed-species grasslands can be. On their diet of grasses, clovers and herbs our eight ewes have no trouble rearing a dozen or so lambs between them. Some have single lambs, some twins. But on average it works out at 1.5 lambs each. A dozen lambs each year amounts to around 240 kilograms of meat. That's from just 1 hectare of natural, species-rich grassland.

No chemical fertilisers required. No pesticides. No purchased cereal grains or compound feeds. No imported soya from land 'reclaimed' by the destruction of Amazonian rainforest. None of the chemical inputs that impoverish so many of today's commercial farmers. It comes as nature's gift to the people of this planet. The product of sunlight, the biochemical pathways of pasture plants, and the ceaseless, unseen activities of the army of living organisms that inhabit fertile soils.

It's a gift of grassland that appears to be universal. A friend of mine – David Lance, a retired farmer from Devon – spent many years developing a profitable grazing system on his small farm near Dartmoor. The farm was organic, and he was determined to use no chemical fertilisers or pesticides. On his natural system he produced 269kg of beef and lamb per hectare.[8]

So what does this mean for our nation's food supply? Government statistics show there are around 7 million hectares of grassland in the UK. This is apart from the farmland we use to grow crops, which is supposed to be the most productive. Grass is grown on land not considered suitable for crops, like my sloping hectare in Somerset and David Lance's land on the edge of Dartmoor. Though most of Britain's pastures will be on better land than ours, let's be conservative and assume every hectare will produce, on average, 250kg of meat a year.

This means that without chemical fertilisers and other damaging pollutants we can easily produce 1.75 million tonnes of pasture-fed meat in the UK, from our grassland alone. Based on a population of 62 million that works out at about 28 kilograms per person a year – or 77 grams a day.

As it happens, this is pretty close to our current red meat consumption of 76 grams a day, as estimated by the National Diet and Nutrition Survey. For men it's a bit higher at 96 grams; for women a little lower at 57 grams a day.

As for how much it's wise to eat, the government's scientific advisory committee on nutrition advises that anyone getting through more than 90 grams of red meat a day needs to reduce consumption. I'm no great fan of these official pronouncements on healthy eating. Many of them turn out to be wrong. But it's clear that using our grassland alone we could produce all the red meat we need, especially if we all ate a little less than now.

So let's celebrate the amazing power of grasslands and their ability to provide us with healthy foods on little but sunlight and rain. It's surely the closest thing we have to a free lunch – a solar-powered food supply mediated through the mysterious life processes of the soil. Eating these foods makes us part of a great interlocking network of life-forms including plants, grazing animals and microscopic organisms below ground. It's the kind of food evolution adapted us for. And that, surely, is the best reason for eating it.

Pasture grazing is a system that works for the world, not just for Britain. Admittedly we have an ideal climate for growing grass – mild winters and plenty of summer rain. But grassland foods are great for arid zones, too. There's no better example than the prairie grasslands that once covered America's heartland, the Great Plains west of the Mississippi. Before the Europeans came along with their repeating rifles and their steel ploughs, these semi-natural grasslands supported an estimated 60 million bison, along with a host of other grazing animals.

In a region prone to drought this was as secure a food supply as you're likely to find. Through a thousand years of drought, fire and storm, the species-rich prairie grasslands flourished. So did the great bison herds that roamed across them in their seasonal migration patterns. So, too, did the herds of Spanish cattle set up by the early ranchers. A couple of centuries on – as corn crops shrivel and burn in the unrelenting sun – many US farmers must wish they could get the grasslands back.

Unlike crop growing, pasture farming doesn't rob soils of their fertility or devastate the microscopic life that sustains it. This is why we don't need new technologies to feed ourselves sustainably. We have the means in the flower-studded green garment that has clothed much of the land surface for millions of years.

While cattle and sheep graze quietly in their unending service to humanity, in today's wheat fields the roar and clatter of machines seldom stops. It's a frenzied dance that leads only to worthless foods and a sterile ground. But there are signs that the dash to crops is faltering. There's a new interest in grassland, especially in the health benefits of grass-fed foods. And nowhere more than in the land that once contained the finest grasslands on the planet.

Halfway through writing this book I Googled the term 'grass-fed' to see what would come up. What came up were just short of 10 million sites. I scrolled through the first few pages. There were fitness sites, healthy eating sites and dozens of farm sites offering grass-fed steaks, grass-fed cheeses and a host of other natural foods.

Something was changing. Tectonic plates were shifting. The land that gave the world fast food, burger bars, fried chicken restaurants and feedlots was now in search of something better.

At the forefront of the movement is a ranch on the plains of North Dakota, a little to the east of the state capital

Bismarck. It holds the promise of better foods and a healthier future whichever side of the Atlantic we live. This farm on the American prairies is proving there's a better way to feed the world, one that's kinder to animals, wildlife and the people who will eat the foods.

In the state that produces half America's durum wheat together with 90 per cent of its rapeseed oil, it's no surprise that Brown's Ranch grows crops, and a wide range of them. What's remarkable is that Gabe and Shelley Brown, who run the place with their son Paul, grow their crops without using the chemical fertilisers, pesticides and GMOs that most American farmers rely on. The Browns don't even use that most ubiquitous of all weedkillers, the increasingly suspect chemical glyphosate.

Included in the farm's cropping list are wheat, oats, maize, sunflowers, peas and lucerne. The sheer diversity of plants on the place is one of the reasons their system works. They manage to achieve high yields and make good profits, despite having kicked out most of the chemicals. Or perhaps because of it. Either way, unlike many of today's farmers, they're producing crops that are rich in nutrients.

The success of Brown's Ranch is mostly down to the traditional fertility-builder – grazing livestock. Their family's main objective is to build deep, fertile soils. And they're using nature's way of achieving this – by covering the land with a rich mix of grasses and herbs, then grazing them with cattle and sheep.

Gabe Brown is a farmer on a mission. In his own words he's set on 'regenerating the landscape'. His aim is to restore health and fertility to a land ravaged by decades of industrial agriculture. In the country where the wild bison herds once roamed across an ocean of natural grasslands, monocultures of wheat and corn now stretch from horizon to horizon.

Another feature of this new prairie landscape are the CAFOs (concentrated animal feeding operations), also known as feedlots. Most American beef, pork and chicken are produced in these 'factory farms'. Thousands – sometimes tens of thousands – of cattle are crowded together in sheds or compounds, and fattened on grain-based rations. They are never allowed to graze fresh pasture.

The feedlot system owes much to the former US Agriculture Secretary, Earl Butz. In the early 1970s he championed a new food production system that promoted grain surpluses.[9] Before Butz, over-production usually led to the government paying farmers to take land out of production. However, Butz saw this policy as interfering with the free market. Instead he urged farmers to plant 'from fence row to fence row', no matter what the need.

Farmers responded by flooding the market with corn (maize), soya and wheat. To compensate them for the resulting low prices Butz introduced public subsidies. The cash was meant to be a temporary measure until overseas markets – especially the Soviet Union – opened up to take the grain surpluses. But as in Britain, the subsidies became permanent and much of the cheap grain ended up in the booming feedlot system. The cheap beef it produced put tens of thousands of pasture-based farms out of business.

Feedlots hasten climate change by pumping huge amounts

of greenhouse gases into the atmosphere, while delivering nutrient-depleted meat to unwitting consumers. To keep disease in check – and to speed the animals' growth rates – antibiotics are widely used in feedlots. An estimated 70–80 per cent of all antibiotics sold in the United States are used for fattening farm animals – cattle, poultry, pigs, sheep and goats.[10]

In 2011 more than half the samples of ground turkey, pork chops and ground beef collected from American supermarkets for testing by the federal government contained antibiotic-resistant bacteria, sometimes called 'superbugs'.[11] According to Martin Blaser, author of *Missing Microbes*, American food producers and pharmaceutical companies claim there's no solid proof that antibiotic-resistant microbes are infecting humans. But there's plenty of evidence, he says, to show the same organisms – with the same patterns of antibiotic resistance – turning up in sick people and in animals fed growth-promoting antibiotics.

Gabe Brown, along with a number of other far-sighted farmers, are putting their livestock back in the environment evolution adapted them for – pasture. Their aim is to rebuild a living landscape from farmland suffering toxic overload. One of the most striking results is the renewal of exhausted soils.

Before the European settlers arrived, the wild prairie grasslands were grazed by vast numbers of animals, among them pronghorn antelope, elk and deer. But it was the immense, wandering herds of bison that did most to shape the landscape and maintain its productive power. In the 1860s, as we've seen, there were an estimated 60 million of them roaming the plains grassland, shaking the ground with their thunderous hooves and scoring deep paths in the earth as they followed their traditional migration routes.

Underpinning all this life and energy were fertile soils. The bison herds grazed in a particular way, bunching together for protection against the many predators of the plains, and grazing unselectively. Typically an animal might take a bite or two from a plant, trample several more, then move on. It could be weeks, months or even a year before the herd returned.

Under this pattern of grazing the prairie grasslands developed an immense diversity of plant life. An intact stretch of tallgrass prairie could contain as many as 400 different species. While grass species contributed most biomass, they were outnumbered four-to-one by forbs – wildflowers and herbs. It was the very diversity of their plant life that made the prairie grasslands so productive, as Charles Darwin predicted in the *Origin of Species*.[12]

Below ground the various species developed huge root systems, each drawing moisture and nutrients from a different part of the soil horizon. The American plains are characterised by low rainfall, so the roots of some prairie plants reach down as far as 10 metres in their quest for water. Around their roots the plants built up a vast reservoir of fertility, a store of nutrients and water to power production without the need for chemical fertilisers or irrigation.

All this was lost when the homesteaders arrived to slaughter the bison and plough up the prairie turf for their wheat crops. For a few decades they harvested bumper crops, cashing in the accumulated fertility of a thousand years of grassland. When it was all used up, the soils literally blew away in the dustbowls of the 1930s. The amazing productivity of the prairie grasslands ended with *The Grapes of Wrath*, John Steinbeck's epic story.

Today the prairie states are occupied by endless crop monocultures. With the soil fertility largely destroyed, they must be goaded with chemical fertilisers, pesticides and irrigation to produce anything at all. The toxic grains that result are then fed to animals trapped in their disease-ridden sheds. It's this meat that goes into American supermarkets and fast-food restaurants.

On the plains of North Dakota, Gabe Brown intends to reverse this story of decline and build a truly sustainable system of farming. This means building up the soil to its former fertility. To do this he's using grazing animals just as nature did. Only this time it's with beef cattle and not bison.

Using electric fencing, the Brown family split up their blocks of grassland into a series of temporary paddocks. There are two main herds – beef cows with their calves and the yearling cattle. Through the season the cattle are moved from paddock to paddock in quick succession, just as the Scot James Anderson recommended more than two centuries earlier. Each paddock gets a large bunch of animals each time, then gets a long rest interval before the animals return.

This system – sometimes called 'mob grazing' – mimics the grazing behaviour of the bison herds. Under it, the pastures gradually become more diverse and the fertility slowly builds. The plants capture sunlight and use it to convert carbon dioxide into sugars, some of which are fed through the roots to feed the microbes of the soil. Carbon that has been lost from the soil over a century of industrial farming is now being returned as soil organic matter. Soon the carbon-enriched land will be ready to grow healthy crops once more.

The Brown family use a number of other techniques for boosting soil carbon. For twenty years they have practised 'no-till' methods, which means they don't use the plough or cultivation equipment before they sow a new crop. As a result the top few centimetres of fertile soil with its precious population of microbes gets minimal disturbance.

The ranch also makes good use of species-rich 'cover crops' on the crop areas. These act as companions to the main cash crop, protecting the soil and helping to enrich it through their root systems. When the cash crops have been harvested, the cover crops are grazed using the same mob grazing techniques as on the grassland areas.

Together these methods have led to a dramatic increase in soil fertility. Two centuries ago, when much of North Dakota was under natural grassland, soil organic matter in the area ranged from 7 to 8 per cent, according to scientists with the National Rivers and Streams Assessment (NRSA). When Gabe and Shelley bought their land back in 1991, tests showed soil organic matter at around 1.8 per cent. In other words, three-quarters of the soil's organic matter (and its carbon) had been lost over the past two centuries.

Today the crop lands at Brown's Ranch show organic matter levels between 5 and 6 per cent. In just over twenty years of mob grazing and other regenerative methods, the amount of carbon and organic matter in the soil has been tripled.

Gabe recalls: 'When we started the depth of black soil on the farm was two to three inches. After that we were in non-fertile subsoil. Now we can dig down eighteen or twenty inches and still be in rich, fertile soil. Grazing livestock have played a key part in this transformation.'

Restoring their soils to health has made farming a lot more profitable for the Brown family. Their grassland will now carry far more cattle than it used to, even though they've stopped putting on expensive chemical fertiliser. Which means they're producing more food for lower inputs. It's enough to put a smile on any farmer's face.

Not long ago I met a Canadian farmer from Saskatchewan who'd been 'mob stocking' his cattle for a dozen years or so. Neil Dennis was making a series of farm visits to the UK, explaining to interested British farmers how his system worked. I caught up with him on a farm in Wiltshire and talked to him about this new-old way of producing food. He told me that adopting a more natural way of managing his cattle herd had changed his life – and his farm.

Since switching to the practice of mob grazing, his farm had come alive. As his soils became increasingly fertile – and as their levels of organic matter climbed – so the land grew a lot more grass. Thanks to the natural grazing system, his farm had become so fertile that it fed four times more cattle than it had at the start.

It's as if he had gained another three farms at no extra cost, Neil quipped to me. His cattle were healthier as a result of their natural, open-air life. He almost never had to assist with calving as he did when they were wintered inside. And as the cattle thrived, the farm's wildlife had proliferated.

'I've never had so much fun in a lifetime of farming', he told me with a twinkle in his eye.

In North Dakota, Gabe Brown has also found that his cattle and sheep stay healthy when they're living the way nature intended. They keep moving to fresh ground so they stay ahead of parasites and insect pests like flies. Just as chemical fertilisers and pesticides are no longer needed to keep crops healthy, Gabe has stopped using insecticides for fly and parasite control. In his wildlife-rich pastures, natural insect predators take care of that. Large flocks of 'cowbirds' follow the herds all year round, keeping fly numbers in check.

But while there are many benefits to the system, the one that really stands out is the difference it makes to the quality of the food we eat. Gabe is convinced that healthy soil will provide clean air, clean water, healthy plants, healthy animals and, ultimately, healthy people. Thanks to the ranch's grazing methods the soil now harbours billions more life-forms that 'feed the food produced'.

Soils that are biologically active produce foods containing higher levels of vitamins and minerals. When we eat these foods these nutrients are passed on to us. The grazing animals that enrich the soil are themselves a healthier source of meat than grain-fed animals kept in sheds. As we've seen, they contain higher levels of health-protecting omega-3 fats, CLA, the cancer fighter, and the antioxidants vitamin E and beta-carotene.

Here's the natural successor to our current industrial farming system that has done so much to contaminate our everyday foods and rob them of their health-protecting properties. At Brown's Ranch – and a handful of other farms across the world – cattle and sheep spend their lives grazing species-rich pastures, moving across the landscape and regenerating soils.

It's a system that replicates the behaviour of the vast herds of bison that once migrated across the North American plains, or the countless millions of wildebeest that still sweep over the African savannah. In Europe the great herds of wild cattle known as aurochs also grazed this way thousands of years ago.

Pasture plants evolved under this intense but intermittent grazing pressure. They became adapted to short bursts of trampling and grazing followed by long rest periods. It was nature's way of sustaining life and enriching the earth. By taking grazing animals out of their natural environment – feeding them unnaturally on grains in sheds and feedlots – we are not only destroying our planet, we are poisoning ourselves.

Gabe has no doubt that we're all suffering the consequences of our destructive farming methods. He says: 'We're spending more money on healthcare than any other country, but look where it's gotten us. The United States is now the 42nd healthiest country in the world. We're first in cancer, autoimmune diseases, attention-deficit disorder (ADD), attention-deficit hyperactivity disorder (ADHD), Parkinson's, Alzheimer's and obesity.

'Why is that? We're degrading our resource [soil] so much that we no longer have the nutrient density in our foods for people to get healthy diets. We need to start thinking of food as health. Good food is preventive medicine. The nutrient density of our foods has decreased anywhere from 15 to 65 per cent over the past 40 years. It can't continue.'

The first figure to recognise the importance of intensive grazing was a Zimbabwean naturalist called Allan Savory. I once went to a talk by this softly-spoken revolutionary during a whistle-stop visit he was making to London. I'd been told that the guy had interesting things to say about grass, and since I'd become something of a grassland geek I made the trip to a small meeting room off the Euston Road. What I heard over the next hour or so blew me away.

Grassland and grazing, said Savory, weren't just useful ways of helping to feed the growing population of the planet. They were, quite simply, the only practical means available for stopping large parts of the Earth's land surface turning into desert.

In his home country of Zimbabwe the young Allan Savory worked as a naturalist and game warden. Africa's game was his passion. So much so that he believed cattle to be the great enemy. It was their grazing behaviour that led to soil erosion and desertification, or so he thought. In an attempt to heal the land he spent a lot of time fencing off large parts of the game reserves so livestock couldn't wreak any more damage.

He was amazed to discover that the fenced-off land deteriorated even faster. Puzzled, he began to look deeper into the issue. How was it, he wondered, that vast areas of the African plains were subjected to intense grazing and trampling during the annual migrations of the great wildebeest herds, only to grow back thicker and stronger than ever?

Like the French biochemist André Voisin, he realised that the answer lay in the length of the recovery period. After their intense mauling under the hooves and teeth of the wildebeest herds, the African grasslands enjoyed a long period of recovery. During this time their diverse plant species could regrow leaf tissue, capture more sunlight and rebuild the reserves of carbon around their roots.

From these observations Savory developed a new paradigm for farming, which he calls 'holistic management'. It's a kind of blueprint based on three distinct principles. The first is, of course, that the farm has to make a profit. The second is to ensure that the farming system is beneficial to the wider environment. The third is that it should take account of the social impact of its activities on farmers themselves, their families, their customers and the community at large.

Holistic management is the system embraced by the new pioneer grazing managers like Gabe Brown in North Dakota. Philosophically it's a million miles from the introverted, reductionist perspective that has led the world down the blind alley of high-input grain growing.

In the state of Virginia, another American farmer has based his successful business on intensively grazed pasture. Joel Salatin's Polyface Farm has become one of the best-known farms in the US ever since *New York Times* writer Michael Pollan featured it in his book *The Omnivore's Dilemma*. I even got in on the act myself when I interviewed Salatin on film while he was in the UK running a course on grazing management.[13]

Salatin believes in basing his farming methods on patterns found in nature. So when it comes to grazing his cattle he borrows from the example of wild grazing herds. The world's great grasslands have been maintained and stimulated over aeons by herds that act in particular ways, he explains.[14]

First, as we've seen, they stay bunched up in a tight group to deter predators. This close grouping means the animals can't be 'picky' about the particular plants they eat. They have to grab whatever's in reach, even if it's only a bunch of thistles. Nor can they be too careful of where they place their hooves. This means that the turf gets well and truly hammered, a process that stimulates biological activity.

Then there's the fact that wild herds move constantly. They are forever in motion, never staying long in the same area. They are always moving onward like some restless, foraging tribe. This endless migration spreads excrement over the whole landscape, says Salatin, while keeping the animals ahead of their parasites and other pathogens. It also provides the pasture with its essential rest period between grazings. Rest periods mean the grass grows better and more carbon is captured in biomass, the total mass of living material.

Finally, there's the key fact that native herds don't eat grain or fermented forages. Nor, it should be added, do they eat distillery waste, fruit syrups, biscuit crumbs, bakery waste or citrus fruit pulp, all materials that are fed to feedlot cattle.

Salatin says: 'The beauty of the herbivore is its ability to turn perennials into nutrient-dense foods such as meat and milk. The unnecessary trappings modern American agriculture hangs around that simple idea are remarkable – ploughing, planting, combine harvesters, grain elevators, feedlots and anhydrous ammonia tanks.

'If we sat down with a committee to try and figure out how to make something needlessly complex and inefficient, the modern confinement, grain-based production model would be a perfect example. But if we concentrate on nature's simplicity based on the behaviour of the wild herds, grazing becomes the most environmentally-friendly food production model possible.'

But could big-scale grazing management have a place outside the great plains of Africa and North America? Could it have a role in the smaller, wetter, more intimate landscapes of western Europe? Someone who is convinced it could is a British estate manager called Tom Chapman.

It would be hard to think of a more unlikely revolutionary than Chapman. Having grown up working on his grandfather's farm in Staffordshire, he took a degree in agriculture and land management at the Royal Agricultural University, Cirencester, before managing dairy farms. He went on to work as farm business advisor for a national firm of accountants, and later to become an agricultural manager with a leading bank.

Today he runs his own consultancy and estate management business in Hertfordshire. Among his core clients are the Bowes-Lyon family, who have a traditional country estate. Chapman's CV doesn't suggest radical change, but he has a vision to transform much of lowland Britain. He wants to see great herds of cattle roaming across the chemical-drenched arable lands, bringing life and fertility back to their tired soils.

With the support of his clients he has begun trialling mob stocking in the fields of his adopted home of Hertfordshire. Although it's too soon to draw any firm conclusions, he says, there are clear signs that the soils are improving and the cattle becoming healthier. That's why he's looking for investors to fund new large-scale grazing operations in the eastern counties of England.

Before developing his plan for a radically-altered countryside, Chapman undertook an intensive study of mob grazing around the world. Carried out under a Nuffield Farming Scholarship, the study took him to Paraguay, Argentina, Canada and the United States. His vision now is of herds of ruminants (cattle and sheep) mob grazing their way across East Anglia, adding natural fertility to the hungry soils and making farming more profitable and sustainable. He might have added that they'd also be making Britain's food supply a lot more nutritious.

In his Nuffield report, Chapman writes: 'Livestock should become an integral part of all arable rotations. To achieve it arable farmers will need to enter business relationships with keen, young farmers looking for a start in the industry.

'By emulating the huge herds of yesteryear, mob grazing encourages grass plants to complete their full life cycles, improving the overall capture of sunlight and greatly lifting the productivity of the land. In addition, mob-grazed cattle trample significant quantities of forage onto the soil surface, feeding the micro-organisms and other soil life. A happy side-effect is that cattle are much healthier.

'Bringing cattle back into the arable rotation offers real financial benefits for the farmer. Soils become more fertile so there are big savings to be made in chemical fertilisers. The soils hold more water, a useful feature both at times of drought and during heavy rainfall. The bottom line is that cattle in the rotation can improve the farmer's bottom line!'

Ohio farmer and writer Gene Logsdon, himself a convert to pasture farming, describes it as the flowering of an 'old-new agrarian way' of producing food. It means relying on grazing animals and pastured poultry to provide meat, milk, wool and hundreds of other animal products at a fraction of the cost of producing them with the current factory technology.

'Pasture farming is the first alternative to high-tech agriculture that has both short-term and long-term profit on its side', he says. He is a passionate exponent of mob grazing. As a producer of low-cost, healthy food, he's convinced it beats grain production hands-down.

'Once the fields of grasses and clovers are established, spring work amounts to turning the animals onto pasture paddocks in rotation and watching them eat', he says. 'Rains don't hamper soil cultivation because there is no soil cultivation. There is no erosion. There are no costly cultivation tools. Hailstones won't hurt the grass. Even flooding only harms it temporarily.

'The animals harvest the pasture crops, control most weeds by eating them, and spread their manure for fertiliser, all without labour, fuel or machinery expense. The amount of fertiliser and herbicides necessary to keep the pasture productive is minimal, and sometimes not needed at all. The farmer mends fences and makes hay.

'You don't have to be a genius to figure out which farming method is more economical – as well as ecologically sane.'

If you want an example of the sheer productive power of grassland, there's nothing to beat the reports of early European travellers on the American plains. The writer Mari Sandoz recalls the experience of Colonel Richard I. Dodge near Fort Worth – later Dodge City – in Kansas:

> At least twenty-five of the thirty-four miles were through one immense dark blanket of buffaloes – countless smaller bunches came together for their journey north. From the top of Pawnee Rock, Dodge could see six to ten miles in most directions, all one solid mass of moving animals. Others who saw the herd reported that it was twenty-five miles wide and took five days to pass at a given point – probably fifty miles deep. Dodge estimated that there were about four hundred and eighty thousand in the one herd: perhaps half a million that he saw himself on that single day. With those that others observed beyond Dodge's sight but still of the same herd, it was estimated at from four million to twelve million counting fifteen head per acre for the former number. This was the great southern herd.[15]

This is nature's productivity. Even as grasslands sustained

these enormous herds of grazing animals, they were helping to regulate the world's climate by storing vast amounts of carbon in the soil. We'd have to be pretty stupid not to harness this power in our food systems.

CHAPTER 7

Grazing animals – our planet's best friends

When you think about grazing cattle it's probably in terms of the harm they're doing to our world. Over the years they've been accused of all kinds of environmental crimes from changing the climate to polluting water and degrading the land.

If you enjoy meat or dairy foods you probably experience the odd pang of guilt. After all, ruminant animals like cattle and sheep burp the greenhouse gas methane, which is known to be 23 times more damaging than carbon dioxide.

The reason so many of us hold these views is mainly down to a 2006 report from the United Nations Food and Agriculture Organization.[1] Called *Livestock's Long Shadow*, it claimed that cattle and other ruminants were responsible for no less than 18 per cent of the world's greenhouse gas emissions.

A few years later the UN moderated its claim. Grazing animals, apparently, can now be blamed for only 14 per cent of global emissions.[2] But it's going to have to go a great deal further. The climate campaigners have ignored a huge environmental benefit of grazing animals. Their calculations were based on faulty carbon accounting.

If they'd looked at what was happening in the real world they'd have discovered that, far from being a threat to our environment, livestock are part of the solution to climate change and land degradation.

They are capable of cutting the greenhouse gas load on the atmosphere far more effectively than smart technical fixes such as wind-farms and carbon 'scrubbers' at power stations. Contrary to what conventional science tells us, the best thing we can do for the planet is release cattle from the sheds where we so often shut them away and put them back on pasture where they belong.

On a windswept plateau high on the Cotswold Hills – the site of an old World War Two aerodrome – a unique farming experiment is under way. Carried out by a softly-spoken Yorkshireman, it has huge implications for the health of all of us.

I met up with farm manager Rob Richmond on a bright, sunny day in early summer. The farm where he works is a long way from the popular chocolate-box image of the Cotswolds with its honey-coloured cottages and drystone walls. To older locals in the nearby village of Chedworth the former aerodrome was known as a tough place to make a living, with its poor, stony soils. But the way it's being run today is proving them dead wrong.

We took a walk up to see Rob's dairy cows, which were gathered at an electric fence waiting to be let through to a new section of pasture. If your picture of a grazing field is something like a lawn, be prepared for a surprise. The area of pasture the cows were impatiently awaiting access to was nothing like our image of well-managed grassland. It was a tangle of tall grasses and flowering plants, some of them half a metre or so tall. Many of the plants were in flower, splashing vivid reds, yellows and blues across the green turf. In the summer sun the air was filled with buzzing bees and flickering butterflies.

Richmond unhooked the fence line, allowing the cattle to flood through the gap onto the new grazing. They tucked into it with gusto, stripping the tender leaves and flowers off tall fibrous stems. In the general melee many plants were trampled into the ground. In conventional farming circles this would have seemed a shocking waste. In fact, most modern dairy farmers would condemn the pasture as a worthless collection of weeds, in which the only worthwhile grasses had been allowed to get far too old and stemmy to be of any nutritional worth.

But to Rob this seemingly wild, wasteful orgy of grazing and trampling is exactly what he has tried to create. He has copied the way wild grazing herds behave, the huge bison herds that once roamed the prairie grasslands of the American Midwest, or the mighty herds of wildebeest that still migrate across the plains of the Serengeti in Africa. The mixture of grasses and herbs he has sown on this high Cotswold plateau is deliberately designed to reflect the botanic diversity of natural American prairie grasslands, before the European settlers killed the bison and sowed the land with wheat.

The resourceful farm manager has gone much further than this. Using the modern device of the electric fence he has recreated the grazing behaviour of the wild bison herds, but with English dairy cows. As we have seen, as a protection against predators the wild herds bunched tightly together and were constantly on the move. Moving along their seasonal migration routes, the animals grazed and trampled the flower-rich grasslands as they went. It might be weeks or months before they returned to an area, giving the grass and herb species a long period of rest to regrow, to flower again and perhaps set seed.

Richmond reproduces this pattern on his Cotswold pastures. The wide expanse of grassland on the high, open plateau is sub-divided by electric fences into a series of small paddocks, more than 40 in all. The 200 or so cows in his herd move from paddock to paddock, grazing off the grasses and flowers as they go.

As soon as they've grazed and trampled one small area of pasture they're moved on to the next. Depending on the time of year, it may be many weeks before they return to a grazed paddock. By then many grasses and herbs will be in flower again, just like those of the now long-destroyed prairie grasslands of the American plains.

To those of us familiar with the British grazing tradition of turning cattle onto a leafy, single-species grassland and leaving them there for days or even weeks, it seems a bizarre and pointless embellishment. But Richmond has discovered that the practice of grazing by 'natural' methods produces extraordinary benefits for the farmer, the consumer and the health of the planet.

Cattle remain remarkably healthy on this system. The frequent movement from one grazing plot to the next means they don't linger on the trampled area with its dung and flies. Their species-rich diet provides a much more balanced package of nutrients, which means they are far less likely to succumb to the chronic conditions that plague many modern dairy herds – mastitis, infertility and lameness.

For consumers the chief benefit, as we have seen, is that mixed grazing diets like this produce meat and milk rich in many of the nutrients that protect human health – omega-3s, fat-soluble vitamins and the cancer-fighting compound CLA.

These are the foods of our distant ancestors. Hunter-gatherer diets were rich in unsaturated fats including omega-3s.[3] Had Rob Richmond's cattle been reared for meat rather than milk, it would have been five to ten times lower in saturated fat than the meat of corn-fed animals.[4] Whoever would be drinking the milk of these contented cows – or eating dairy products made from it – would enjoy similar benefits.

But there's another advantage of this 'designed with nature' pattern of grazing – it builds up amazing levels of fertility in soil. When the European settlers ploughed the ancient American grasslands in the later 19th century, the soils they opened up contained huge amounts of carbon. This was held in both living organisms – the numberless mass of bacteria, fungi, protozoa, nematodes, earthworms and the rest that make up the subterranean population – and in a complex group of organic compounds known collectively as humus.

Many of the soils under natural, tallgrass prairies were made up of 15 per cent or more organic material, equivalent to almost 9 per cent carbon. Under our current, chemically-driven crop farming, the level of soil organic matter is less than one-fifth of this. The missing soil carbon is now in the atmosphere adding to our climate-change woes.

No wonder there's a new generation of far-sighted American farmers who want to turn the clock back, or rather turn it forward to a new grazing age. If the arid prairie land can produce healthy meat without chemicals or subsidies – and at the same time capture large amounts of atmospheric carbon – you'd have to be mad not to do it.

The new graziers point to the North America before the Europeans came. Pre-Christopher Columbus the American plains were home to an estimated 60 million bison – with each adult animal weighing a tonne – along with 40 million pronghorns, 10 million elk, 10 million mule deer and perhaps 2 million mountain sheep.[5] All these ruminant animals were pumping out methane, yet there was no global warming. Through natural processes the carbon in the methane was finding its way back to the soil.

Soil microbes played an important part in these processes. Healthy soils contain a group of microbes known as methanotrophs, which use methane as their sole carbon and energy source. In some soils they are able to significantly reduce methane concentrations, though nitrate fertilisers, pesticides and other farm inputs reduce their activity.[6]

Grazing animals play a key role in regulating the carbon dioxide content of the atmosphere through the use of soil as a carbon sink. It's a natural process that has been going on for millions of years. Yet unaccountably we have decided that livestock should be imprisoned in sheds and yards, while we ruin the life of our soils to feed them.

Biologist and environmentalist Allan Savory believes the campaign against grazing animals poses as big a threat to the future of humanity as does our profligate burning of fossil fuels. Across vast areas of the planet where life is dependent on seasonal rainfall, grasslands are turning into deserts. This is because the vegetation – and the fertile soils that sustained it by storing water – were created by the great wild herds of grazing animals.

Now those herds have gone, and over much of the world's grasslands soil organic matter – and carbon – is being lost. So the vegetation is dying and the land is drying out. The social consequences in many areas are hunger, poverty, violence, social breakdown and war.

In his online TED talk,[7] which when I last looked had received more than 3 million views, Savory described how managed grazing was restoring life and health to around 15 million hectares of threatened grassland on five continents. In doing so it was giving hope to the people who lived there. Incredibly, if these techniques were practised on just half the world's grasslands, they would take enough carbon from the atmosphere to return our planet to pre-industrial carbon dioxide levels, while at the same time producing healthy food.

'I can think of almost nothing that offers more hope for our planet, for your children, for their children, and all of humanity', says Savory.

But can the grazing pattern that restores soil life in the world's dry grasslands do a similar job in cool, rainy Britain? On the farm he runs on the Cotswolds, Rob Richmond is discovering that it can. By planting species-rich grassland in place of the usual grass monoculture – and copying the grazing patterns of the wild bison herds – he's finding he can put carbon back into the soil at an extraordinary rate.

When he took over the management of Newport Farm back in 2004 most of the fields had less than 5 per cent organic matter in the top 15 centimetres of soil. In some fields it was as low as 2 per cent, which is standard for much of Britain's intensive arable land.

Today all the fields at Newport Farm are up at around 10 per cent organic matter. Some have gone from 2 per cent to 10 per cent in less than a decade, an extraordinary rate of accumulation. Much of this is in the top few centimetres. But with deep-rooting herbs in the pasture, Richmond is hoping there will be carbon accumulation lower down in the soil, where it's more likely to be stored in a stable and long-lasting form.

He estimates that about half the carbon captured or 'sequestered' will be converted by soil fungi to stable humus compounds. According to Richmond it takes around 60 tonnes of carbon as humus to raise soil carbon – and organic matter content – by one percentage point over a hectare. Under his natural grazing management this appears to be happening in about three years.

What this means is that if all Britain's livestock were reared this way we would remove carbon from the atmosphere at a rate equivalent to half the nation's total emissions. In practice the benefits might be even greater. If we reared grazing animals solely on their natural food, grass, we'd be growing far fewer cereal crops with their heavy requirement for fossil fertilisers and pesticides. We would, in fact, far exceed our carbon emission targets.

At the same time we'd benefit from healthier, more nutrient-rich foods and a production system that was genuinely resilient. Soils high in organic matter would store large amounts of water, protecting our food supply in periods of drought. And when rain came in deluges – as the climate scientists say is likely to happen with increasing frequency – we'd have a food production system that also protected us from flooding.

It seems an extraordinary idea. Grazing animals, reviled by the UN for the damage they're supposedly doing to the world's climate, turn out to be the solution to some of our most intractable challenges. Cattle, managed in ways that mimic the grazing patterns of wild herds, can clean up our atmosphere as part of the natural process that stores carbon in soils. And in doing so they put nutrients back in our foods and make farming profitable again.

It's a claim that still leaves mainstream soil scientists sceptical.[8] But out there in the real world pioneering groups of farmers are discovering it works.

At the forefront of the movement is an Australian soil ecologist called Christine Jones. For two decades or so she has been working with a large group of farmers to restore life to soils wrecked by years of following conventional, chemical-based farming methods. The results they've achieved are astonishing.

On one Australian farm the amount of carbon sequestered has averaged an incredible 33 tonnes of carbon dioxide equivalent per hectare each year. Three-quarters of this is in what's called the non-labile fraction of the soil. This means it's highly stable and will not easily oxidise and be lost again as carbon dioxide. It adds up to a near-permanent cleaning up of our atmosphere.

Christine Jones and the farmers she works with have achieved these results by concentrating on a part of the global carbon cycle that has largely been ignored by conventional science. She uses the phrase 'liquid carbon' to describe the transfer of organic compounds from plant roots to soil microbes. Their subterranean interactions lead to the build-up of humus, the durable, complex group of compounds containing about 60 per cent carbon.

In the global carbon cycle, carbon exists in three distinct phases, says Jones: as gas, as liquid (in plants) and as a solid.[9] The threat facing humanity is that much of the carbon that was once in solid form – in the soil – is now in the atmosphere as gas. This is dangerous for the human species. Climate change is only part of it. Food security, the nutrients in our food, and the capacity of our soils to hold water are all reasons for keeping solid forms of carbon in soil.

Modern chemical agricultural methods interrupt the flow of liquid carbon from plants to soil. Cultivations, pesticides and chemical fertilisers all break the network of mycorrhizal fungi, key players in the transfer of carbon compounds from plant roots to soil microbes. As we saw earlier, plants secrete these carbon-containing 'exudates' in order to attract the microbes they need to populate the area around their roots. It's these microscopic soil populations that will feed the plants, supplying the dozens of nutrients they need to grow and stay healthy.

But when plants can easily obtain essential nutrients like nitrogen and phosphorus in the form of chemical fertilisers, they stop pumping out carbon. Conventional farming with its pesticides and fertilisers is inadvertently breaking the vital microbial bridge. Robbed of their carbon supply, microbial populations diminish and die. Soils lose their structure and are eroded away.

When you look at the beauty and complexity of these natural systems, the use of grazing animals in our food systems starts to make sense. The rotational grazing of species-rich pasture results in more carbon being sequestered than is emitted as methane. Compare this with the carbon footprint of fuel, fertiliser, weedkillers and pesticides needed for the production of grain-fed meat.

Factor in the soil erosion, water contamination and emissions of carbon dioxide and nitrous oxide that are the price we pay to grow grains or soya, and the grass-fed approach looks like the only carbon-friendly option. Add in the health advantages of grass-fed meat and dairy foods, and our present food system starts to look serially stupid.

In Australia chemical farming has done huge damage to soils that are inherently less stable than those in Europe. As their soils have become impoverished, farmers have found it harder than ever to make profits. This is why a growing number of them are looking for new, more productive systems of agriculture.

One of the more promising of these is known as 'pasture cropping'. It does away with ploughing and the separation of fields into arable and grassland. Instead annual cereal crops are planted directly into a pasture using a special seed drill.

The cereal crops grow during the period when the pasture plants are dormant. When the crop's harvested the pasture plants start growing. These are then grazed by cattle or sheep until it's time to plant the next cereal crop. Several hundred Australian farmers are now using the system. They've found that it produces huge benefits for their profits and the environment.

New South Wales farmer Colin Seis has been using the system for more than fifteen years. He has found he can grow cereal crops for a fraction of the cost of growing them conventionally. This is because the pasture supplies the growing cereal crop with most of the nutrients it needs, so he doesn't need to apply much chemical fertiliser. And as well as harvesting a profitable grain crop, the farmer also gets a second crop from the same land: the meat or milk from the grazing animals.

But perhaps the biggest benefit of the system is the extraordinary amount of atmospheric carbon it locks up in soil organic matter. Christine Jones, as founder of Amazing Carbon, reports that in the ten years to 2010 the system on Colin Seis's farm locked up a total of 164 tonnes of carbon dioxide per hectare. In the final two years of the decade – the soil having grown more fertile – it was locking up (sequestering) an incredible 33 tonnes of carbon dioxide each year, as we saw earlier.[10]

Results like these are jaw-dropping. If all the world's cereal crops were produced this way we would easily reach the world's global carbon emission targets without resorting to untried and costly technologies. Plus we'd all enjoy healthier foods. Yet the policy-makers along with the scientific establishment continue to ignore the power of grazing to restore our planet to health.

Christine Jones blames this ignorance on the classic models for soil carbon dynamics. These are based on data collected from conventionally-grazed, chemically-fertilised pastures. Under these conditions the bridge between plant root and soil microbes is dysfunctional, she says. When this link is restored, soil fertility – and the nutrients available to crop plants – rise dramatically.

'The puzzle is that establishment science clings to these outdated models', she says, 'inferring real-life data to be inconsequential. Measurements made outside of institutional science are dismissed as anecdotal and largely ignored. When pastures are managed to utilise nature's free gifts – sunlight, air and soil microbes – to form new, fertile, carbon-rich topsoil, the process is of immense benefit to farmers, rural communities and the nation.'

To Rob Richmond it's a no-brainer. In his view it's high time we threw out the chemicals from food production and moved to an agriculture based on sound biology. What makes his argument so convincing is that it comes, not from a theoretician or an idealistic dreamer, but from a hard-headed, profit-minded, down-to-earth farmer who has to make things work – and pay – in the real world.

Rob grew up on the family dairy farm in Yorkshire, then took a degree in animal science at Edinburgh University. As a farm manager he has worked on a number of dairy farms, most of them with large, conventionally-run herds. He's seen a dairy industry where mastitis, infertility and lameness are rife, and where farmers have come to rely on vaccines, drugs and chemicals just to keep things going. Richmond calls these 'rescue remedies'. To him their universal use shows something is deeply flawed in the current production model.

Modern science seemed to hold few answers for Rob. In fact modern science with its close links to the chemical and pharmaceutical industries was the reason these damaging systems had come into being. So he began looking into the experiences of a past generation of farmers and scientists. In the mid-20th century – around the time chemical fertilisers were beginning to find favour with agricultural scientists and the farming establishment – there was a spate of new writing about biological methods of food production.

Many of these new writers were highly sceptical about the chemical approach. They feared the new products that seemed to promise so much in yield and output would do long-term damage to soil fertility, with disastrous consequences for humankind. More than half a century on, their fears are proving to be all too well founded. To Richmond this meant their ideas were worth looking at again. If these methods worked then, they would work today. Nature plays no games.

The books he read are the books I remember from my own student days. They're written by very different people from a range of backgrounds and with a variety of experiences. But there's a common thread to all these ancient narratives. They all tell of the extraordinary productive power of soils when their microbial populations are allowed to flourish.

There was Sir Albert Howard, the distinguished scientist, who showed that crops grown on soils rich in humus were always better than those raised with the aid of chemical fertilisers.[11] It's only when plants are nourished with the aid of soil fungi that they can resist disease organisms and produce healthy, nutrient-rich crops, Howard revealed.

In *Food, Farming and the Future*, published in 1951, livestock and racehorse breeder Frank Sykes wrote of his experience of transforming poor land on the edge of Salisbury Plain into a highly productive farm using 'humus farming' alone and rejecting chemical methods. Referring to the microbial life of the soil he says: 'These organisms need to be increased if the minerals of the soil are to be made available for our use and living. But they cannot be increased or maintained in good health unless they are adequately fed with supplies of humus, provided by intelligent farming.

'In this way more food will be made available, land will rise in fertility and disease will diminish. The peace of the world can be ensured, for contentment will follow the provision of adequate food.' In the language of the mid-20th century it sounds like a pious hope. Yet, as we've seen, more than 400 scientists and development experts have come to a very similar conclusion – biological methods are the best, and perhaps the only way to feed the people of this planet.[12]

These stories made increasing sense to Rob Richmond in his search for a better system than he'd seen on many dairy farms. He was pleased to discover that the biological systems which promised healthier crops and animals were also likely to mean better profits for the farmer. For instance, in a book published more than a century ago, Roxburghshire farmer and former tea planter Robert Elliot wrote that farmers had no need of chemical fertilisers.

The cheapest soil conditioner was a turf made up chiefly of deep-rooting herbs such as chicory, which pushed their roots deep into the ground, breaking up any compacted areas that prevented air and moisture getting to soil microbes. Plant roots, wrote Elliot, were far and away the best tillers, drainers and warmers of the soil.[13] They were nature's own fertilisers.

At the time Elliot was writing in the 1890s, Britain was awash with cheap food imports. In those days the competition for British farmers came mostly from the unexploited soils of the Empire, the prairie wheat lands of Canada and the fertile grasslands of New Zealand and South Africa. Britain, the great industrial power, relied on her manufacturing industry to pay for food imports.

But the day would come, Elliot warned, when countries like China, Japan and India would emerge as powerful industrial nations. To survive in this new competitive world, Britain would need to make better use of her most valuable resource, her herb-rich grasslands and their ability to produce strong livestock and health-giving foods. The constant reliance on artificial fertilisers would cost farmers dear. It would empty their bank accounts and exhaust the soil.

The common thread in all these writings was the idea that soil fertility was the key to animal and plant health. Building fertility meant relying on the microbial life of the soil, not on chemical fertilisers. Much of this has now been forgotten, though with the chemical approach clearly failing, these natural methods made good sense to Rob Richmond. But before trying them out on the farm he wanted to learn from the experiences of farmers in other parts of the world.

He applied for – and was awarded – a Nuffield Farming Scholarship to look at a different way of farming, one based on rebuilding soil carbon. He travelled first to the United States, home of GM crops and large, intensive animal operations, but which also supports a thriving ecological farming movement. He then went to Australia where poor soils, an arid climate and the absence of government subsidies have led farmers to look for cheaper ways of producing food.

Together these influences have totally transformed Richmond's ideas about farming. He uses no pesticides or chemical fertilisers at Newport Farm. Instead he relies on fertile, carbon-rich soil to feed his cows and produce healthy milk. Unlike the short, leafy grazing pastures of most British farms, his grazing paddocks, with their tall, flowering herbs, look a lot like America's tallgrass prairie grasslands before the European settlers got there.

As we saw earlier, a small patch of tallgrass prairie – the vegetation in the wetter eastern region – might easily have contained as many as 400 different plants, most of them non-grass species or forbs. These wildflowers and herbs occupied the spaces between grass plants, boosting soil fertility by bringing up nutrients from deep down in the soil, and, in the case of legumes, by 'fixing' nitrogen from the air.

A metre-square section of tallgrass would have an underground network of roots and root hairs that, placed end to end, would stretch twenty miles. Two-thirds of the plant biomass of prairie grassland lay below ground. There the dense network of roots was constantly being renewed.

The European settlers changed all that. Within a few decades of their arrival the grasslands and the buffalo had gone. In their place the farmers sowed wheat, the new Turkey Red variety which was tough enough to withstand the harsh prairie climate. For the prairies the coming of annual crops spelled the end of the land's amazing productivity.

It came as a great shock to 1930s America to see the billowing black clouds drifting across their cities; clouds not of smoke or water vapour but of soil particles. Today the prairie lands are still under crops – corn and soya mostly – but only because they are constantly dosed with chemical fertilisers and pesticides, and because the US government is prepared to spend billions of dollars a year on irrigation and public subsidies.

Fly across modern America and everywhere you'll look down on rivers that run the colour of local soils. This is erosion by water. Lifeless soils, poisoned by chemicals, are washing away in the rain, taking their nutrients and their pesticides downstream to the sea. The run-off of nitrate fertiliser from farmland is responsible for the single largest source of nutrient pollution, causing the massive 'dead zone' in the Gulf of Mexico.[14]

⇻⇺

One of the worst cases of soil erosion I've seen was in a country lane near Worcester as I drove to meet a UK-based environmental expert called Dave Stanley. The red silt was several centimetres thick at the roadside where it had been deposited by some recent torrent and left to dry out. It formed a narrow strip of beach along 200 metres or so of the lane. In places it was wide enough for a couple of deckchairs, and at one point a small volleyball court. And as Stanley later told me, this was after the local council had already hauled away several truck-loads of the stuff.

Dave's explanation was clear and uncompromising. The soils were washing away because intensive agriculture – particularly intensive crop production – had robbed them of the organic matter necessary for the characteristic 'crumb structure' that gave them life and vitality. During decades of chemical farming, organic compounds had oxidised, releasing their carbon into the atmosphere as carbon dioxide. There was now an urgent need to reverse the process and put more carbon back into the soil. That meant a fundamental change in the way we grow our food.

You can't help but agree with this energetic northerner whose enthusiasm for the subject seems to know no bounds. For a start he is a certified environmental auditor and Fellow of the Institute of Environmental Management and Assessment.

He has also done a spell of farming, in a small way admittedly, but enough to convince him that agriculture holds the key to many of the world's most intractable problems.

But perhaps the chief reason you're inclined to accept Dave Stanley's nostrums is that he has had a distinguished earlier career as a fast-jet pilot. He flew both Hunters and Harriers for the Royal Air Force. As he explained to me, when you're flying a Harrier your effectiveness in carrying out a mission – not to mention your own personal safety – depends on understanding the machine as an entire system.

The habit of so many experts to concentrate on some small part of a complex system wouldn't work when it comes to flying fast jets. You need to have a clear grasp of how the whole process works. Today Stanley uses that same holistic approach in his investigation of greenhouse gases and climate change. It's led him to very different conclusions to those arrived at by most policy-makers in this area.

Climate change is believed by many scientists to be caused by the accumulation of carbon dioxide in the atmosphere, mainly as a result of human activity. Over the past two centuries atmospheric carbon dioxide levels have gone up from 280 parts per million to 365 parts per million. To avert climate disaster the policy-makers recommend measures to reduce carbon emissions. But this approach makes little sense, says Stanley, when you understand the whole carbon cycle.

As we sit drinking tea in his cottage near Worcester he helpfully brings me up to speed with the basics. Governments and climate change experts talk of the need to reduce carbon emissions to the atmosphere even though they know this is technically difficult and politically unpopular. Yet the biomass – the sum total of vegetation covering the planet – holds almost twice as much carbon as the atmosphere, while the world's soils hold three times as much. The actual amounts are constantly in flux as carbon is transferred between these three sinks by the natural processes.

So doesn't it make sense to maximise the transfer of carbon from the atmosphere into the great repository of the soil? No new technologies are required. It's what traditional farming communities have been doing for thousands of years. As farmers like Rob Richmond are showing, it's possible to capture carbon at a rate that far exceeds carbon emission targets and, at the same time, to produce healthier, nutrient-rich foods and protect against flooding and drought.

As Stanley puts it, rather than pursue 'no carbon' strategies the world needs to adopt a 'carbon max' policy, with the max applied to the amount of carbon held in the soil. Sadly, he doesn't see much chance of such a policy being introduced any time soon. Crop yields per acre have stagnated over the past ten years, principally because on crop-growing land soil carbon levels have fallen to the point where they are nearly dysfunctional, between 1 and 2 per cent.

The UK government seems to recognise there's a problem. Its current 'Safeguarding our Soils' strategy acknowledges that intensive agriculture has degraded soils and that they are at risk from erosion and further organic matter loss. There are hints of improved soil protection and new goals 'to reduce the rate of loss of stored carbon'. But there's no sense that the policymakers know there's a tried and tested solution out there.

On the small farm he used to run in Lincolnshire, Dave Stanley learned first-hand the power of pasture and livestock to restore worn-out soils to health. His policy was to raise beef cattle using the local Lincoln Red breed. He grazed them on pastures that ranged from traditional meadowland to new grassland sown on land that had been previously used for chemical crop production. The soils beneath the various pastures all varied in their carbon content. But under grazing, carbon levels rose by around one percentage point in eight years, equal to an organic matter increase of 1.7 per cent.

This is rather less than farm manager Rob Richmond achieved with his pasture paddocks full of deep-rooting herbs. But even using conventional grazing methods Dave discovered that grasslands can efficiently capture carbon and, at the same time, produce nutritious food. The refusal of scientists and policy-makers to recognise real-world events is costing us all our health and our environment.

To Dave Stanley the UK government's response to soil degradation has been next to useless. It has put in place an 'evidence-based investment strategy'. But while accepting that intensive agriculture has degraded soils, it has allocated just £1.7 million to soil protection and £4 million to water protection. Aerospace research, by contrast, gets £150 million annually in subsidies. Once more, corporate profits come way ahead of human health.

Soil needs to be at the heart of UK environmental policy, says Stanley, particularly in relation to climate change. Currently most effort goes into reducing carbon emissions to the atmosphere, even though atmospheric carbon totals just

800 gigatons, while the world's vegetation holds 1,500 gigatons. But the world's soils hold a massive 2,500 gigatons of carbon.

This is why it makes sense to concentrate on maximising the carbon content of soil rather than on reducing emissions. And the much-abused cow is the most effective way we have of doing this.

From his new home close to the River Severn, Dave Stanley, the former fast-jet pilot, now produces slow food – grass-fed beef. He rears native-breed Lincoln Reds solely on flower-rich meadow grazing with hay in winter. He produces some of the healthiest meat around, high in omega-3s. He's also maintaining a natural system that keeps our planet alive. Not a bad tale to tell the grandchildren.

CHAPTER 8

In search of real milk

The winter of 2014/15 was a bad time for dairy farmers, or so the media claimed. The prices paid for their milk were down by about a quarter on the previous year. This resulted in a big fall in profits, with some farmers losing money on every litre produced.

According to the *Daily Mail*, it was 'the worst crisis ever'. Britain's dairy industry was hanging in the balance, said a story in the *Guardian*. It noted that the number of UK dairy farmers had halved in the last decade and was now down to fewer than 10,000. Writing in the *Daily Telegraph*, a National Farmers' Union spokesman said being a dairy farmer was like being a boxer – you're on the ropes and taking body blow after body blow.

The print media treated the crisis like some sort of Shakespearean tragedy. *Guardian* leader writers extolled the dairy industry as one of the great influences shaping the British countryside and rural life. It had helped create the patchwork of small fields and hedgerows. It had sustained family farms over generations. It had created a distinctive pattern of country lanes and hamlets. There was even a fond reference to Tess of the D'Urbervilles taking her milking stool out into the Dorset meadows.

So far so predictable. But how much had the dairy industry contributed to its own demise? Since the first Neolithic herders trekked with their livestock across grasslands reclaimed from forest, the people of this land have produced milk from cows grazing on pasture. Grass is both the cheapest and the best food for dairy cows. It also produces the most nutritious milk.

But after decades of market protection, the industry seems to have forgotten this simple reality. Farmers have managed to build in a battery of extra costs that don't need to be there – chemical fertilisers, pesticides, massive machines, big sheds and acres of concrete. This is why many of them are finding themselves uncompetitive in an unforgiving global market.

But there's a way back for those bold enough to take it. They can once more put grassland at the heart of their businesses. If enough of them do so they'll bring our countryside back to life while making a big contribution to the nation's health.

'Proper Milk' read the hand-painted sign at the side of the quiet Suffolk lane. I felt a small tremor of excitement. Proper milk isn't something you find much of in today's Britain. I turned off the lane and drove down a rutted track. It ended in a concrete yard beside a large, open-fronted barn. As I stepped out of the car I knew I'd come to the right place. On the far side of a low brick wall a small group of Jersey cows grazed contentedly on a pasture full of clovers and herbs. Their milk was going to be something very special.

I'd arrived at the aptly-named CalfAtFoot Dairy. It's called that because, unlike modern commercial dairy farms where calves are snatched from their mothers when they're just a day or two old – causing great stress to both – these calves stay suckling their mums for at least nine months. On the day of my visit there were three calves running with the small herd.

Behind the name and the unusually humane system of milk production was the woman I'd come to see. Fiona Provan, first-time farmer and passionate animal welfare campaigner, has been a *cordon bleu* cook and seller of high-quality street food. But since childhood, when she lived next door to a dairy farm and helped run her father's veterinary practice, her greatest ambition has been to look after cows. The dairy business she's set up in Somerleyton near Lowestoft on the Suffolk/Norfolk border looks set to be a game changer for the industry.

When I called at the farm she'd been running CalfAtFoot Dairy for about two years. Establishing it was a brave move. Though she hopes to make a decent living from the business, her production methods have little to do with the supposed 'economic realities' that are driving most dairy farmers to build ever-bigger herds and to squeeze every last drop of milk from each over-worked beast.

Fiona is guided by one overriding principle that comes way ahead of profit. The welfare of the cows is her first priority. Her whole system is built around the need to give her beloved animals happy, healthy lives. They'll eat their natural foods out in the open air, as nature intended. And they will never suffer the trauma of having their calves snatched off them at just a day or two old.

As it happens, this principled approach to dairy farming may also turn out to be a profitable one. A growing number of people are discovering that milk produced this way – and drunk raw – has many health advantages over the pasteurised, homogenised, standardised and generally over-processed version on sale in supermarkets.

As I write this, Fiona is selling her top-quality milk direct from the farm at £3 a litre, well above the supermarket milk price. To the dozens of committed customers who drive down the rutted Suffolk lane each week it's a small price to pay. They are convinced that this wholly natural product will protect their health in a way the conventional version can't.

It's why price comparisons with the white liquid sold in supermarkets are meaningless. What Fiona is selling, in the view of many, is a real food containing a host of health-protecting nutrients. The supermarket version is often priced below the cost of bottled water. So it's hardly surprising that many dairy farmers see it as a cheap commodity to be produced at the lowest possible cost.

Today full-fat milk is shunned by healthy-eating enthusiasts. But a century ago a diet of raw, whole milk was widely recommended as the cure for a range of conditions including diabetes, gastric ulcers, obesity, and kidney disease. In the United States a physician called Charles Sanford Porter published *Milk Diet as a Remedy for Chronic Disease*, a book that ran to eleven editions. In it he wrote: 'A good food is also a good remedy. Disease is simply a disturbance of the mechanism of nutrition. So it's natural that the use of milk in ill health is almost as old as its use as a food.'[1]

Porter insisted that the milk should be raw and unpasteurised. In 1929, Dr J.R. Crewe of the Mayo Foundation in Rochester, Minnesota published an article on the benefits of milk.[2] In it he claimed to have used unpasteurised milk to improve a variety of health conditions, including obesity, heart disease, diabetes, prostate enlargement, tuberculosis, and high blood pressure.

Modern science has begun to support some of these early health claims, especially when the milk and dairy foods are produced in the traditional way from cows grazing on fertile, fast-growing pastures. Cows are adapted to eating grass. It is their natural food. Evolution has equipped them with a large fermentation chamber, the rumen, in which fibrous materials, low in energy, are broken down by resident micro-organisms. This is, after all, why human beings domesticated them in the first place. Ruminants have the capacity to convert inedible roughages into food.

In Europe, cows were traditionally calved in spring. So the peak demand for milk came at the time when the growth of fresh green grass was at its most vigorous. Many mountain peoples, like those of the Bernese Oberland in Switzerland, placed a special value on the intense yellow butter made from the milk of cows feeding on this early spring grass. They believed that its life-enhancing qualities were especially beneficial to children and expectant mothers.

Milk from cows feeding on young, fresh grass contains high levels of the fat-soluble vitamins A, D, K and E. So butter made from this milk is a rich source. As we've seen, milk from grass-fed cows also contains high levels of essential fatty acids, particularly omega-6 linoleic acid together with CLA, with its strong anti-cancer properties.[3] Even small amounts of milk and cheese from pasture-fed cows have been linked to a significant fall in the cancer risk.[4]

CLA is produced in large amounts by cows eating fresh, green pasture.[5] But when cows are fed on small amounts of grain, or even on grass that has been cut and conserved in the form of silage, its level in milk falls away dramatically.[6] And as with beef there's evidence that traditional pastures containing plants like plantain, self-heal, rough hawkbit, red clover and bird's-foot trefoil produce milk with higher CLA levels than even all-grass pastures.[7]

Research at the University of Aberdeen showed that levels of omega-3 fats were, on average, 30 per cent higher in organic milk than in non-organic milk.[8] But the differences were far higher in the summer months when the organically farmed cows had greater access to fresh grass and clover-rich pastures.

Without the benefit of modern scientific knowledge the traditional dairy farmers of Europe knew their summer pastures delivered the healthiest and most nutritious dairy foods. It's a belief that persisted well into the 20th century.

Sadly, dairy farming has now been transformed from a natural process into a largely industrial operation. Together the dairy industry and the supermarkets have worked to undermine the traditional benefits of milk. Between them they've turned a real food into a cheap commodity depleted of many nutrients. They've done it because of a farming obsession for 'yield', the volume of milk that can be extracted from each cow.

In the 1960s, the average British dairy cow produced a little over 3,500 litres a year. Today, the average is almost double this, with some high-production herds notching up 10,000 litres or more. The cow is able to transfer only so many nutrients to her milk. The greater her milk volume, the more dilute its nutrient content, particularly for vitamin E and beta-carotene, a precursor of vitamin A. The traditional cows may have put less milk in the tank at the end of every day, but while they were grazing fresh pasture it was milk packed with nutrients.

The modern Holstein super-cow is little more than a walking milk factory. Grass, the natural food of ruminants, is unable to meet the energy and protein needs of these high-performance animals. Hard-wired to produce milk at the expense of their own bodies, they require nutrients in concentrated form or they will break down their own body tissue to the point of collapse.

No longer can they be allowed to graze pasture for much of the year. Grass – if it's part of the diet at all – must now be supplemented with a range of industrial feeds, many of which spoil the nutritional value of the milk. Grains such as wheat, maize and barley are among the starchy foods chosen to boost energy levels in the diet of high-yielding cows. These industrial crops are cheap and plentiful. But there are other, equally damaging foods on offer: potato waste; bread discarded by the factory bakers; breakfast cereals that for one reason or another have been rejected for the human food chain.

These energy-rich foods have to be 'balanced' with feeds supplying concentrated protein. Today, farmers rely heavily on soya meal to supply protein in concentrated form. Unfortunately most soya, like cereals, is grown with heavy inputs of pesticide and chemical fertiliser. Other widely used protein feeds include groundnut meal, rapeseed meal, and cottonseed meal.

On modern factory farms, grazed grass produces, on average, less than one-sixth of the milk that goes into the food chain. The rest is produced from other feed materials. That's why our dairy foods no longer have the health-giving properties of those from traditional farming systems based on flower-rich pastures.

The healthy omega-3 fats of grass-fed milk are largely eliminated on these industrial rations. These high-octane dairy rations also depress the levels of CLA in milk, so reducing its protective effects against cancer. Fat-soluble vitamins are reduced; so are the antioxidants lutein and zeaxanthin.

The modern, intensively-farmed dairy cow is herself far from healthy. Starchy grains in the rumen increase the acidity in this fermentation chamber. The rumen microbes react by producing an excess of lactic acid, some of which is absorbed into the bloodstream where it plays havoc with the animal's normal metabolism.

Toxins are also released into the bloodstream. These are produced by the decay of micro-organisms killed off in the over-acid conditions. Dangerous pathogens can take their place, seizing the new opportunity and multiplying rapidly.

Infections of the udder are common in the national herd.[9] Routine antibiotic treatments are used during the 'dry' period

– the few short weeks of the year when cows are not lactating. Many of today's dairy cows suffer from lameness, commonly caused by a restriction in the blood supply to the feet. As if this weren't enough, the stresses on these high-performing animals have led to high levels of infertility.

Many of today's intensive dairy cows are worn out by the time they've reached their third lactation cycle. By contrast, cows grazing naturally on clover-rich pastures for much of the year – like those at CalfAtFoot Dairy – can stay productive for ten years or more.

Together the costs of fertilisers, big machines, diesel fuel, purchased grains and the sickness they cause all add a huge cost burden on modern dairy farming. It's the reason why today's dairy farmers struggle to make a living. Their businesses are weighed down with unnecessary costs.

The industrialisation of milk production has brought few benefits for dairy farmers. Today, they're getting out at an unprecedented rate. In the early Seventies there were 100,000 dairy farmers in Britain. Nine out of ten of them have now gone and the drop-out rate is increasing. Small, family farms have been among the hardest hit, not because they are any less efficient at producing milk, but because their overheads – items like rent and labour costs – are higher.

Those that remain are turning themselves into factory-scale operations. Many modern dairy units are little more than a collection of industrial sheds, surrounded by acres of concrete and lit by security lights.

These are no longer farms. They are more like rural factories. 'Get bigger or get out' is the background refrain of bankers, accountants, management consultants, and the vast army of advisors who have their own reasons for seeing farming behave like any other business. But dairy farms have never been like other businesses. They are a key part of Britain's story.

Neolithic herders may have been the first dairy farmers, but their semi-nomadic way of life flourished again through the custom of the shielings, widely practised in Britain's hill country, whereby cows were moved to upland pastures in summer.

In Shakespeare's time it was dairy products that sustained poor families when the price of bread rose too high. An acre or two of pasture would feed the house cow of the lowly peasant or 'cottager', keeping the family supplied with milk, butter and cheese throughout the year, whatever the price of bread.

Centuries later the coming of the railways gave dairy farming a further boost. In the mid-19th century a growing demand for fresh milk was chiefly being met by 'town dairies'. These were small herds kept in dark cellars and fed chiefly on used brewery grains, bakery waste and the 'cake' left over from oilseeds after the oil had been extracted. The quality of this town milk was generally poor. Hygiene standards were non-existent.

But the new railway branch lines returned dairy farming to the countryside. Farmers who somehow managed to get their milk to a railway station could get in on the fast-expanding urban market. The Duke of Buckingham even built his own private railway to take the milk and butter from his tenant farmers to Quainton station, part of the rail network.

With pasture-fed milk on offer, city families couldn't get enough of it. In the final quarter of the century, UK milk consumption rose by nearly two-thirds. One contemporary writer – John Sheldon – described the new 'milk trade' as 'the most remarkable phenomenon in the history of agriculture'.

Grass-fed milk remained the norm until the mid-20th century. On the Thames Valley farm where I worked as a student in the 1960s they ran a dairy herd. The 30 or so Friesian cows were Jim the herdsman's pride and delight. Under his watchful eye they'd spend the summer months grazing lush, clover-filled pastures. In return they rewarded us with the richest, creamiest milk I've ever tasted.

My job was mainly as tractor driver on the arable land. But when Jim needed help to fix a fence or move a bunch of heifers I'd be expected to drop everything and lend a hand. Afterwards there'd be a glass of that special milk taken fresh-chilled direct from the bulk tank. To me the flavours of that soft, pastoral landscape were as distinct as the *terroir* of any French wine or artisan cheese.

In those days dairy farming was the jewel in Britain's rural landscape. Out in the fields cows were mostly the classic native breeds – Jersey, Ayrshire, Guernsey and Dairy Shorthorn – breeds that had become famous around the world. The British Friesian was becoming increasingly popular.

More than any other rural enterprise it was the family dairy farm that pumped money into the local community, keeping village schools and shops alive. It was dairy farming, too, that helped maintain our glorious pastoral landscape of small fields and hedgerows.

Today the connection with that chequer-board field pattern is looking increasing fractured. A growing number of farmers are scaling-up the size of their herds and keeping them in large sheds. As we've discovered, instead of chewing on the grasses, herbs and hedgerow shrubs evolution prepared them for, they eat mixed rations containing high-energy maize silage and cereals, along with protein-rich foods such as soya.

To be fair, many dairy farmers feel they no longer have any choice in the matter. They feel they're being pressed like some gigantic Cheddar cheese – and turning the screw are the supermarkets and the big milk processors.

The social and economic forces that have downgraded British milk are also at work in the United States. There, too, herds have grown larger, cows are increasingly kept in 'confinement' rather than outside on pasture, small family farms are being driven to the wall. Food campaigners have had enough. They're intent on turning the tide, and the method they've chosen is modelled on a small revolution that took place in the UK.

In 1999, the Weston A. Price Foundation of Washington, a non-profit-making organisation set up to disseminate the discoveries of the nutrition pioneer, launched 'A Campaign for Real Milk'. It was inspired by a group of English blokes who sat in a pub back in the 1970s and bemoaned the rise of the corporate brewers and the threat to British ale. Out of that meeting sprang The Campaign for Real Ale (CAMRA), the movement that saved traditional beer.

According to the Real Milk Campaign website: 'Back in the 1920s, Americans could buy fresh raw whole milk, real clabber [curdled milk] and buttermilk, luscious naturally-yellow butter, fresh farm cheeses and cream in various colours and thicknesses. Today's milk is accused of causing everything from allergies to heart disease and cancer, but when Americans could buy Real Milk, these diseases were rare. In fact, a supply of high quality dairy products was considered vital to American security and the economic wellbeing of the nation.

'What's needed today is a return to humane, non-toxic, pasture-based dairying and small-scale traditional processing.'[10]

Ron Schmid, naturopathic physician and author of *The Untold Story of Milk*, writes of buying 23 acres of land at Watertown, Connecticut, land that had once been a small dairy farm.[11] With partner Elly, the plan was to stock the farm with a few hens, plus six to eight Jersey cows, and begin supplying grass-fed raw milk, meat and eggs to the local community. It's a step he'd like to see duplicated thousands of times across the length and breadth of America.

'What the dairy industry has striven mightily to eradicate – wholesome milk and independent dairy farmers – is growing up like new grass on a spring morning', he writes. 'Every week hundreds of consumers discover that raw, whole milk products from grass-fed cows represent the answer they are seeking to their health problems; and every week dozens of farmers wake up to the fact that the direct sale of raw milk, raw cheese, raw butter and raw cream is the answer they were looking for, the way to save the family farm.

'Raw milk is the key to the health crisis, the farm crisis, the economic crisis, the small town crisis, even the environmental crisis.'

Eighty years earlier an English farmer beset by the same difficulties came to a similar conclusion. Threatened by low prices and cheap imports, Arthur Hosier took the radical step of keeping his dairy cows outdoors on his rolling chalk downland for 365 days a year, even milking them outside in mobile milking units.

Though the land was cold and exposed, the cows were expected to stay out on pasture all year round in all weathers. Despite the climate they remained remarkably healthy under their 'free-range conditions', quickly adapting to the outdoor life by growing long, thick coats. At the same time they stayed free of the crippling ailments that plague modern dairy farms – lameness, infertility and udder disease.

They didn't seem to contract tuberculosis either. In the 1920s TB was rife in the human population, with tens of thousands dying from it every year. Many were believed to contract the disease from contaminated milk. But in their healthy, outdoor conditions Hosier's cows never developed TB. Even 'reactors' – cattle giving a positive result in TB tests – failed to develop the disease when brought on to the farm. He claimed: 'If all cows were kept in the open air on dry land and properly fed, tuberculosis would be non-existent in five years.'

Keeping cows outside on pasture dramatically cut Hosier's production costs, enabling him to make good profits while other dairy farmers were struggling to break even. What's more, the milk he produced was purer and healthier than most other milk around. In a speech to the Farmers' Club in London he said: 'Milk produced from cows living in the open air is better in every respect. It is of much higher food value than milk produced in stalls [inside]. It keeps longer, and is higher in butterfat. Infectious diseases of the udder are almost unknown.'[12]

Hosier delivered his speech in 1927 when the world economy was in recession and farmers were struggling to make a living. He showed that by producing healthy milk from pasture, and selling direct to the public, there were good profits to be made.

Over the next few years a small number of farmers adopted the system. By 1930 a total of 86 had taken up 'open air' dairying, producing between them enough milk to supply a city the size of Leicester. Two years later a team of economists from Oxford University carried out a study of over 70 open-air herds. They concluded that in many parts of Britain the future of dairy farming lay in the adoption of these simple, open-air methods.

Had Hosier's revolution continued we'd all now be enjoying a wonderful, health-giving food. Unlike today's milk it was so pure it didn't need heat treatment to make it safe. This meant it retained its full complement of nutrients, including vitamins, enzymes and protective fatty acids. It would have helped prevent many of today's most crippling ailments

– heart disease, many cancers, osteoporosis, arthritis and asthma.

Sadly it wasn't to be. The big dairy companies convinced the government that the only safe milk was milk that had been heat-treated. In effect this meant farmers could no longer sell their milk direct to the public, no matter how pure it was. Instead it would have to go to one of the dairy companies for processing. The dairy industry had effectively taken control of the nation's milk supply.

Despite the clear health benefits of pasture-fed milk, dairy farming has since gone in precisely the wrong direction, as we've seen. Herds have got bigger and cows have been concentrated in ever larger numbers inside sheds, where they're fed diets containing large amounts of industrial grain.

It's almost impossible to buy healthy milk in today's supermarkets or, for that matter, from the home delivery floats of the major dairy companies. It's true there are still a number of pasture-fed herds dotted around the British countryside. But inside the stainless steel silos of the dairy companies this good milk is swamped in the deluge from farms that fill their cows with cereal grains and soya. Even the so-called healthy milks are spoiled by the standards of their poorest producers.

Despite these changes – or perhaps because of them – dairy farming found itself back in crisis. The government pledged support. Environment Secretary Liz Truss said she'd help farmers sell dairy products to China. There was talk of an EU 'futures' market for dairy products, allowing milk to be traded in advance, giving farmers greater long-term price security.

Some in the industry talk openly of more 'restructuring'. Their argument is that the dramatic fall in dairy farm numbers hasn't led to shortages. Instead production has been concentrated into bigger herds. The process needs to continue, they claim, so Britain ends up with a truly efficient dairy industry. In other words, milk production must become a large-scale factory operation rather than a farming enterprise.

But there's an alternative. A growing number of dairy farmers are finding that by making the best use of pasture they can reclaim that most elusive prize in milk production – profit. Two West Country farmers – Neil Grigg and Tom Foot – have established a large dairy herd that stays outdoors all year round.[13] The cows are milked once a day through a portable milking parlour designed and built by Tom from an old milking frame found abandoned in the hedge.

In a reinvention of Hosier's methods of the 1920s they are producing high-quality milk at very low cost. They're able to sell it at a premium price to a nearby cheese company where milk of this quality is highly valued.

The West Country duo are currently building up their outdoor herd to 800 cows. At the other end of the size scale, new farmer Nick Snelgar has developed a small mobile milking unit along with a pasteurisation (heat treatment) plant suitable for a small farm.[14] He has also built up a flourishing market for local milk in the homes and shops close to where he lives in the village of Martin in Hampshire.

Nick has discovered there's a keen demand for grass-fed local milk. He has found that at the prices people are prepared to pay, a herd of no more than twenty cows can provide a decent income for a new, young farmer. He hopes the development will open the way for thousands of micro-dairies around the country in the same way that micro-breweries have taken off.

Could pasture-based production lead to a new golden age for UK milk, just as it did in the 1920s? Not everyone's a fan of milk, even the grass-fed sort. Loren Cordain, author of *The Paleo Diet*, argues that dairy foods have taken a heavy toll on human health over the past 9,000 years or so. The fatty acids they contain – palmitic acid and myristic acid – raise blood cholesterol, he argues. They also increase the risk of developing heart disease and other chronic illnesses.

By contrast, the Weston A. Price Foundation – the nutrition foundation set up to promote and continue the work of the healthy-eating pioneer – recommends whole milk, cheese and butter from grass-fed animals. It adds that all these foods should be eaten raw and unprocessed. In traditional societies, dairy foods were often fermented so they provided plenty of enzymes to aid digestion.

From her big barn in rural Suffolk Fiona Provan is one of a handful of UK pioneers aiming to put real milk back into our impoverished diets. As we sat drinking coffee at her desk – just a few metres from where her beloved Jersey cows are milked each morning – we talked about her hopes for a dairy farm revolution in Britain. She's counting on a popular demand for real, healthy milk leading to the nation's cows being released from their sheds and put back on the pastures where nature meant them to be.

For the moment she's working on proving her humane,

low-cost system of milk production as a realistic business proposition. As a way of producing the best milk around, it clearly works. Farmers have been doing it for 9,000 years. But she's keen to show that direct selling to consumers can make the CalfAtFoot Dairy a sound business idea. Once she's done this, her aim is to help others set up similar dairies around the country.

Bring it on, I say. The NHS figures show there's not a moment to lose. Britain needs this real food back as quickly as possible.

I once knew an old dairy farmer called Jack who milked a small Jersey herd in a beautiful valley in Wiltshire. At the age of 80 he still led his beloved cows to their summer grazing each morning. Science now shows this milk to be the best for health, while economists say it's the most economical to produce.

If we don't allow a new generation to go on farming this way, it's hard to see how we can call ourselves either food-lovers or countryside supporters.

CHAPTER 9

Wild new farms

I well remember the moment when it finally came home to me that Big Wheat posed an existential threat to our countryside. I was at an open day to celebrate a new nature reserve at Parsonage Down, just along the road from Stonehenge in Wiltshire.

The previous owner of the land, farmer Robert Wales, had died a few years earlier at the age of 93. Throughout his long life he had farmed the flower-filled chalk grasslands in the traditional way, by grazing them with cattle and sheep. While most of his neighbours had ploughed up the ancient turf to grow wheat in return for generous EU subsidies, he was determined to go on doing what he thought was best for the land. And that meant grazing it.

As a result, chalkland flowers that long ago became scarce on the downlands still grew in abundance in his fields. They included devil's-bit scabious, toadflax and green-winged orchids, together with cowslips and salad burnet. In summer those same fields became alive with butterflies, bees, grasshoppers and crickets. Willow warblers haunted the gorse bushes and brambles; stone curlews called in the evening air.

When Farmer Wales died, this ancient beauty was at once under threat. Under the EU's Common Agricultural Policy there were generous subsidies on offer to anyone ploughing up pastures like these and sowing the land to wheat. Not that anyone needed the wheat. There were already large and embarrassing surpluses across Europe. Much of the grain mountain was destined to be sold off cheap to the Soviet Union. As in the US, wheat surpluses had become an instrument of global politics.

Fortunately Robert Wales had foreseen the danger. Under the terms of his will the land was offered to the nation at barely one-fifth of its value on the open market. But the new Thatcher government was not in favour of the state acquiring national treasures – at least, not of this sort. If a new nature reserve was to be established on the farm it would have to pay its way.

To protect at least some of the flower-rich grassland, the rest would have to be sold on the open market to cover the full cost. On the day the deal was due to be completed, tractors were queuing up in the lane ready to put the priceless turf under the plough.

As an act of sheer vandalism it was like taking half a dozen of Turner's masterpieces out of the National Gallery and torching them on the pavement of Trafalgar Square.

Modern, industrial agriculture has been a catastrophe for Britain's wildlife and wild places. As mentioned in Chapter 4, intensive arable cropping is reckoned to have led to the decline of half of plant species, one-third of insect species and four-fifths of bird species on farmland.[1] The ending of mixed farming and its replacement with intensive cropping areas and intensively managed grassland areas has drastically reduced the wildlife of our countryside.

Though the use of nitrogen fertilisers on grasslands is thankfully in decline, their continued high use on crops has had devastating effects on wild plant species and on the insects and animal species that depended on them. Pesticides, too, have taken a heavy toll on the life of our countryside. The chemicals that accumulate in the food chain – particularly those affecting hormone balance – pose a long-term threat to birds, amphibians and fish.[2]

While the European populations of common and forest birds fell by around 10 per cent between 1980 and 2006, populations of farmland birds fell by 48 per cent.[3] The decline in farmland birds was far higher in the countries with more intensive agriculture.[4]

In the UK the 2013 population of farmland birds was less than half its 1970 level, as estimated by the Farmland Bird Index.[5]

But the losses aren't simply measured in statistics. Our countryside is a collection of special areas; of small, intimate spaces each known and loved by a few people. Intensive agriculture has waged war on them. It has caused the mass destruction of millions of hedgerows, copses, flower-rich meadows, wet grasslands, ponds, scrubby areas and marshes. Every unrecorded loss is a tragedy. And the greatest tragedy is that generations will grow up never having known them.

The justification for all this destruction has been that more production was needed to feed a hungry world. This was the constant chant of the agribusiness lobby as the flower-filled fields of Parsonage Down went under the plough in the early 1980s. It remains as shrill today as an unholy alliance of scientists, biotech companies and farmers lobby for the introduction of GM crops into our toxic fields.

Only now we know it's a lie. A large body of the world's scientists and experts tell us that this kind of farming can't feed the world. It's the system itself that poses the main threat of world hunger.[6] The destruction of so much of our once-glorious countryside turns out to have been pointless. The sheer waste of it all is clear for everyone to see each time one of our great rivers is stained the colour of topsoil.

In the early 1990s, when the destructive forces unleashed by EU farm subsidies were becoming obvious, a rescue plan for wildlife was introduced. Under so-called agri-environment schemes there would now be additional subsidies for farmers who took small parcels of land out of intensive production and managed them for wildlife. The UK currently spends around £500 million a year on these schemes.

Measures include wildlife margins around the edges of wheat fields. Here perennial grasses and wildflowers escape the crop sprayer and fertiliser spreader, providing refuges for invertebrates and food sources for birds and small mammals. Similar refuges – known as beetle banks – are used to break up large areas of arable monoculture.

Sadly these schemes add up to little more than window dressing. They don't address the real problem – that the farming system itself is destructive of life. While these small, semi-natural oases may protect and feed wildlife species, they do nothing to protect the human species whose foods are grown on the tired and toxic spaces that make up the bulk of our crop lands.

The disappearance of birds and other wild populations from the countryside isn't the price we pay for a safe and secure food supply. It doesn't indicate an efficient farming system. It's a clear sign that farming is in deep trouble. When birds disappear from our farmland it's a safe bet that the soil's in a bad way too. That's the real threat to our food.

In 1940, the Medical Research Council published the results of a survey into the nutrient content of many everyday foods. The authors were a doctor, R.A. McCance, and a nutritionist, E.M. Widdowson. Their studies were continued over the next 51 years and were eventually taken over by the Ministry of Agriculture. During this period a total of five reports were published of the McCance and Widdowson results.

Known as *The Composition of Foods*, the dusty reports show how mineral levels in many everyday items have fallen during a period of intensive chemical farming. The finding was made by David Thomas, a geologist who later trained as a nutritionist. He discovered that between 1940 and 1991 vegetables had on average lost 24 per cent of their magnesium, 46 per cent of their calcium, 27 per cent of their iron and no less than 76 per cent of their copper.[7]

The results for two main dietary staples were even worse. Carrots lost 75 per cent of their magnesium, 48 per cent of their calcium, 46 per cent of their iron and 75 per cent of their copper. The traditional 'spud' lost 30 per cent of its magnesium, 35 per cent of its calcium, 45 per cent of its iron and 47 per cent of its copper.

According to Thomas, you'd have needed to eat ten tomatoes in 1991 to get the amount of copper a single tomato would have supplied in 1940.

The results for other produce were scarcely more comforting. Among seventeen varieties of fruit, the contents of both magnesium and calcium were 16 per cent lower in 1991 than they had been in 1940. The zinc content was down by 27 per cent, the iron content by 24 per cent and the copper content by 20 per cent. Even meat showed a fall in mineral levels. In a range of ten popular cuts the iron content fell by 54 per cent and the copper content by 24 per cent.

American researcher Donald Davis, a retired biochemist at the University of Texas, came to similar conclusions. He compared the nutrients in US crops between 1950 and 2009. He found there had been a significant decline in the levels of five nutrients in various fruits including tomatoes, eggplants and squash. For example, there was a 43 per cent fall in iron content and a 12 per cent decline in calcium. An earlier study he'd made on vegetables showed a 15 per cent fall in vitamin C and a 38 per cent drop in levels of vitamin B2.[8]

The response of food scientists is that even if nutrient levels have fallen it doesn't matter much. Foods are now bred for yield, they say, not necessarily for nutritional content. But as people eat a wider range of foods than ever before, there's not likely to be a dietary deficiency.

It's an attitude that neatly sums up all that's wrong with farming today. This is an enterprise dedicated to producing more and more at ever lower cost, regardless of quality. It's a culture that runs deep in the world of subsidised agriculture.

It's also at the heart of food retailing, where a handful of giants engage in a ruthless struggle for market share and survival. What it amounts to is a senseless race to the bottom.

It means the young mum, who has fought hard to get her kids to eat a few greens or carrots, has been cheated. She has been duped into buying dysfunctional foods grown on sick soils. The tragedy is that the missing nutrients could so easily be put back into our everyday foods.

In Chapter 5 we met John Reeves, the retired farmer who became convinced of the vital role played by one particular group of soil organisms. Without them, plants can't take up the minerals they need, so the animals, and people, eating them are more likely to become sick. It's a group of organisms that industrial agriculture has done its best to obliterate. They're the thread-like fungi known collectively as mycorrhizal fungi, which form symbiotic links with plant roots.

There are thought to be seven groups of the fungi, most of which are specialised for particular plant families. The largest group are the vesicular-arbuscular mycorrhizae (VAM), so called because they form little sac-like structures – or arbuscules – inside the root cells. These increase the surface area across which the plant can trade nutrients for minerals.

VAM can increase the absorbing surface of the plant's root hairs by up to 100,000 times. And they can enhance the uptake of soil nutrients such as phosphorus, zinc, copper and magnesium by up to 60 times. That's why these little-known organisms are so essential to human health.

Mycorrhizal fungi are thought to have evolved more than 300 million years ago, in evolutionary terms not long after the appearance of land plants. They evolved to form symbiotic links with the roots of most plant species.

Biologists have known about them for a century. Because of the power of the chemical industry they've been largely ignored. But thanks to the conviction and dogged determination of a scientific amateur, the human cost of that neglect is becoming clear.

Working as a journalist, I heard about John Reeves's work and managed to track him down in a tucked-away cottage on the edge of a small community in the Forest of Dean in Gloucestershire. He told me of the dozens of experiments he'd carried out on plant minerals. His aim was to find out how the presence or absence of mycorrhizae in the soil affects the mineral content of the crops it grows. He admitted to having been sceptical at the start. The idea that a soil fungus could have a significant influence on the nutritional quality, as well as the yield, of a crop seemed fanciful.

But he was a sceptic no longer. He became convinced we'd never again eat healthy foods until we returned to a system of farming that protected these valuable organisms. And that meant getting rid of most of our chemical fertilisers and sprays.

He carried out his experiments on a number of different soils, though many were done on his own land, a magnesium limestone soil to the south of the Forest of Dean. He enlisted the help of a university chemist to carry out the mineral analyses on his plant samples. A sympathetic scientist at

Rothamsted experimental station in Hertfordshire supplied the inoculum of mycorrhizal fungi.

Reeves devised his own mineral score-sheet to represent the overall content of fourteen essential trace elements, including boron, cobalt, copper, iron, magnesium, zinc and selenium. He included in his trials a range of everyday vegetables: carrots, peas, onions, parsnips, potatoes and broad beans.

When the vegetables were grown on cultivated soils without chemical fertilisers their mineral scores were satisfactory, though not high. But when they were grown on soils that had been treated with chemical fertiliser, phosphate, they contained up to a quarter fewer minerals.

Inoculating soils with mycorrhizal fungi had the opposite effect: the mineral scores soared. Comparing the two treatments, vegetables grown on soils with healthy populations of mycorrhizae contained up to two-thirds more minerals than those from soils fertilised by chemicals.

Reeves also looked at a number of farm crops, including wheat and pasture grass. As with vegetables, both the physical act of cultivating the soil and the application of chemical fertilisers destroyed mycorrhizae and depleted growing crops of minerals.

With wheat, he found that soil cultivation reduced the mineral content of grain by a quarter. Putting on chemical fertiliser reduced mineral levels still further, but when the cultivated soil was inoculated with mycorrhizal fungi it again grew wheat containing the full complement of minerals.

Reeves made similar observations of pasture grasses. Grass leaves taken from long-established pasture contained high levels of essential trace elements, but when soils were sown back to grassland after five years of cultivation for crops, the resulting grass showed far lower levels of minerals. Selenium was reduced by half, boron and molybdenum by around 40 per cent, cobalt and copper by 30 per cent, and manganese and nickel by 20 per cent or more.[9]

Farmers knew for centuries that the best way to stop soils becoming exhausted was to grow a wide range of plant species. Monocultures robbed soils of their fertility so the foods they produced were depleted of nutrients. It's the reason biodiversity was a key feature of traditional farms. No farm could be truly sustainable without it – as modern science is only now confirming.[10]

In Victorian times, farmers in Hampshire routinely included twenty or more different crops in their rotations.[11] These included wheat, barley, oats, turnips, swedes, leguminous (nitrogen-fixing) plants such as red and white clover, sainfoin and vetches, as well as cabbage, mustard and kale. Grazing pastures also included a wide range of species, including a number of different grasses plus leguminous species such as clover, yellow trefoil, alsike, and winter and spring vetches. Long before the age of nitrate fertilisers, these plants were putting large amounts of naturally-produced nitrogen into farming systems.[12]

All these crops were grazed with sheep, mostly the local Hampshire Down breed. In a system known as 'folding', they were penned in small, portable enclosures that were moved from one crop to the next over the season. The sheep stayed remarkably healthy on their varied rations. And the growing crops, with their varied rooting structures, passed carbon compounds to different groups of soil microbes. The whole system kept the soil fertile for year after year, decade after decade. It was a truly sustainable way of producing good food.

At that time 'good husbandry' was deeply ingrained in farming culture. Tenant farmers often had to sign contracts undertaking to maintain the diversity of crops. They also had to agree not to grow crops in monoculture, since these would 'exhaust the soil'. This meant farms were full of wildlife. At the same time they were highly productive in crops and meat that were rich in health-protecting nutrients.

According to farming historian Bethanie Afton, these methods worked because they recreated the advantages of the species diversity found within mature ecosystems.[13] The sheer range of crop species meant that they had a measure of protection from pests and diseases. Only in modern monocultures can disease sweep through a crop, making the constant use of pesticides unavoidable.

Ironically it was the introduction of chemical fertilisers that destroyed these sustainable, wildlife-friendly farms. Then, as now, they slowly robbed soils of their life and fertility. In evidence to the Royal Commission on Agriculture in 1895, it was suggested that 'for some reason which is difficult to discover, the quality [of produce] shows signs of deterioration'. Among the explanations given was the 'gradual exhaustion of the fertility of the soil by "whipping" it with artificial fertilizer'.[14]

Half a century later, a Somerset farmer came to the same conclusions about farm chemicals. Frank Newman Turner, whom we met in Chapter 6, was the author of a 1950s classic called *Fertility Farming*. Having rejected chemical fertilisers and pesticides as harmful to his livestock and to his land, he began exploring the links between biodiversity and human health. Instead of nitrate fertilisers he relied on organic compost made from farm animal and vegetable wastes. He also sowed his pasture fields with a mixture of more than twenty plant species.[15]

As we saw, Turner found that by grazing his cattle on mixed, mineral-rich pastures grown on truly fertile soils he could prevent and even cure many crippling diseases that still plague cattle today, including tuberculosis, infertility, mastitis and Johnes disease.

So confident was Turner in his methods that he went round local livestock markets in search of sick animals, especially those he thought might be suffering from TB. He felt sure his pastures would put them right, returning them to health and production and making a few pounds for him.

What Turner may not have known was that his 'herbal leys' were very efficiently feeding the soil microbial population and pumping carbon back into the soil. The deep-rooting herbs such as chicory and dandelion are especially good at promoting long-term carbon storage at lower soil levels.

Chemical farming has robbed soils of their diversity and our foods of nutrients. There's only one way to put both back. That's to increase diversity above ground. It means ending our fixation with monoculture and allowing a thousand flowers to bloom across our wasted farmland. Key players in this transformation will be leguminous plants, those that work symbiotically with soil microbes to fix their own nitrogen.

Research into the role of legumes in raising soil fertility shows that Victorian farmers had most of the answers. In mixed-species grasslands, plants such as red and white clover, bird's-foot trefoil and sainfoin are able to produce huge amounts of nitrogen by natural, biological processes.[16] They have the potential to greatly reduce farming's dependence on fossil fuels, reducing greenhouse gas emissions and nitrate pollution.

Some legumes – including bird's-foot trefoil – contain compounds that help to keep animals healthy. They're known as secondary metabolites. It's worth remembering that grazing animals evolved to flourish on mixed-species grasslands, not on modern grass monocultures.

Legumes also provide farmers with a home-grown source of protein so they don't have to import soya, some of which is grown on land reclaimed from rainforest.

But the greatest advantage of legumes in mixed-species pasture is that they supply carbon compounds to soil microbes. This gives them a big role in the restoration of life and vitality to our damaged farmlands.

On a small organic farm near Northleach in Gloucestershire, farmers Jonathan and Mel Bunyee are using this tried and tested method to boost the biodiversity of their land and produce nutrient-rich foods. Since taking over the farm they have converted a sizeable block from arable to species-rich limestone grassland.

They've done it by sowing seeds of native grasses, herbs and wildflowers into the fields. No sprays or artificial fertilisers have been used. Nor has the plough. Over-sowing of seeds into the former corn stubbles, along with natural regeneration – the emergence of seeds lying dormant in the soil – have been the main agents of change. Also playing a part are the farm livestock – rare Cotswold sheep, the breed once known as the Cotswold Lion, and the original horned breed of Hereford cattle.

Mel and Jonathan, who are tenant farmers on the National Trust-owned Sherborne Park Estate, have also planted herbal leys at Conygree Farm, which takes its name from the Anglo-Saxon word for rabbit warren. As well as grasses, these mixed-species leys contain clovers, deep-rooting chicory, sainfoin, trefoil and plantain.

Mel explains that the leys are well suited for grazing with sheep and have natural compounds that protect animals against parasitic worms. So there's no need to use environmentally-damaging commercial wormers. The legumes also enrich the soil, while chicory helps improve soil structure.

Along with flower-rich field margins at Conygree, the grasslands provide insects and ground-nesting habitats for birds. Flocks of over a thousand finches have been known to feed on the small farm over winter. Species include yellowhammer, linnet, chaffinch, greenfinch and corn bunting.

The couple view the birdlife of the farm as a sort of flying litmus test revealing the health of their bit of countryside. Without the farm's rich biodiversity, the bird populations would be in decline. So would the farm's ability to grow good food. Farmland biodiversity and healthy foods are linked.

Beef and lamb sold from the farm are raised solely on pasture, with no grain fed at any time in the animals' lives. Known as Pasture For Life, the principles of the system were developed by the Pasture-Fed Livestock Association. At Conygree, the sheer variety of herbs, legumes and grasses in the pastures is said by customers to make the meat exceptionally succulent and sweet-tasting. It should also be exceptionally rich in nutrients. These are the kinds of meats we humans evolved to eat. They're from a diverse ecosystem with high carbon levels and a flourishing population of soil microbes. The land is gathering strength.

There's one more element that can make our farms even more productive and our food more nutritious – trees. A report published by the Royal Society argues that land used for animal production could be both productive and richer in biodiversity if trees were added to farmland.[17] Silvopastoral food systems, combining trees and pasture, are good for wildlife and animal welfare, say the researchers. They are also profitable for farmers and truly sustainable, while many modern livestock systems are not.

It's clear we can start to heal the land by enriching the biodiversity of our farms. This will, at the same time, improve the nutritional quality of our foods and diets. For our health – and for the health of our society – it's time to adopt a way of life better-attuned to our hunter-gatherer origins. To eat really well, perhaps it's time our farms recreated the forest ecosystems that are our best guarantee of good health and vitality.

It's a fine spring day in late April and I'm taking a country walk in West Sussex, just to the south of Horsham. The fields I'm walking over are officially classed as farmland, but this is nothing like the farmland we're used to. There are grassland areas, but not the sort we see all over modern Britain. These contain a wide variety of herbs as well as grasses and clovers. There are woodlands too, along with expanses of scrub, where shrubs and young trees have sprung up from their carpet of grass. There are also many mature trees, in small clumps or strung out along the line of an overgrown hedgerow. Others stand in solitary splendour, the monarchs of their small corner of England.

Together the different vegetation types make up an extraordinary landscape. There's something of the ancient forest about it. To me it's reminiscent of the New Forest in Hampshire, that hunting playground of the Norman kings. Through the trees I catch a glimpse of red deer grazing in a grassy glade. Later I spy a group of Longhorn cattle browsing on the leaves of young willow trees that have sprung up in a marshy field.

This mosaic of woody spaces on the Sussex Weald makes up a unique experiment in ecology. Twenty years before my visit this land was in intensive crop production. Each year it was receiving the full battery of chemical sprays and fertilisers. Today the landscape has been 'rewilded'. Grazing animals – Longhorn cattle, red and fallow deer, and Exmoor ponies – roam freely. So do ginger-coloured Tamworth pigs.

Though pigs are mono-gastric animals (with a single stomach) and not ruminants, they, too, often graze when given the opportunity. It's the grazing habits of all these species that decide which vegetation patterns will emerge and become dominant in each area.

The experiment covers the greater part of the Knepp Estate at West Grinstead, an area of heavy clay soils crossed by the River Adur and some of its tributaries. The Wildland Project is the inspiration of owner Charlie Burrell. His first idea was to recreate the original landscape – as set out by the designer Humphry Repton – around the present Knepp Castle, which was built for the Burrell family in 1806 by the architect John Nash.

But the idea grew into a far bigger project – the creation of a landscape-scale 'wildland' in which a variety of large herbivores would roam freely. As far as possible they would be 'de-domesticated'. The plan was to create natural grazing conditions with as little human intervention as possible. Veterinary attention would be given when necessary, and at times of severe weather extra feed would be put out. Otherwise the animals would be left to fend for themselves, very much as they would have done in the wild.

Fifteen years into the experiment it's producing a wealth of data for wildlife ecologists. Scrub fields and unkempt hedges have created ideal conditions for dozens of bird species. The turtle dove – a bird forecast to become extinct in England by the year 2020 – is thriving at Knepp. In the summer of 2015 a dozen breeding pairs were reported. A decade earlier there had been none.

Nightingales are also doing well. In one area – known as the southern block – no fewer than 42 breeding pairs have been reported. At the start of the project there were just nine. More than 50 bird species now breed at Knepp, including long-eared owls and ravens. Ten of the breeding species are listed as of 'high conservation concern'.

Butterflies, too, are thriving on the landscape created by grazing animals. Even after a year of atrocious weather, butterfly specialists counted more than 25 species. The rare brown hairstreak now breeds at Knepp. The purple emperor population is now the largest in the UK. Among other exciting developments are the arrival of peregrine falcons, a boost in the numbers of soprano pipistrelle and Bechstein's bats, plus the discovery of hazel dormice and the rare fungi *Phellinus robustus* and zoned rosetta. Since the choking grip of industrial agriculture has been lifted, this small corner of the English countryside is beginning to breathe again. Wildlife flourishes. The long decline in biodiversity has been reversed.

Underpinning these dramatic developments are changes in the soil. With the ending of decades of chemical assault, subterranean life is now flourishing. The unseen interplay of soil organisms is quickening. Plants of all kinds produce sugars and pass them to soil microbes at their roots. Deer and cattle feast on the foliage, not simply grazing on the grasses and pasture plants, but pulling leaves from shrubs and low trees. With a huge diversity of vegetation on offer they're able to eat selectively, choosing whatever they need to stay healthy. Evolution has prepared them for this, but modern farmers seldom give them the opportunity.

Fascinating though the wildlife developments may have been, for me one of the most interesting aspects of this unique project is what it says about our food and the way we currently produce it. Here are cattle and deer flourishing in as near-natural a grazing system as it's possible to imagine.

No longer are they forced to eat from a heavily fertilised field sown to a single variety of agricultural grass. They're selecting from the pasture plants, shrubs and trees that were likely to have been growing on these clay soils 10,000 or more years ago. So the meat they produce must be pretty much like the stuff consumed by our hunter-gatherer ancestors. Could this be a model for the way we'll produce food in the future? With a landscape designed to keep people healthy by recreating the ecosystem we evolved as part of?

On my spring walk in this newly-created 'ancient' landscape I have two companions – Knepp Estate owner Charlie Burrell and biologist and ancient tree expert Ted Green. Ted is a founding member of the UK Ancient Tree Forum and a long-standing conservation consultant. He's been involved with the Knepp wildland project from its very start, and is keenly interested in soil fungi. This is because he knows them to be vital to the health of the trees he cares about. He's equally sure they're important for human health too.

We walk through the mosaic of woody spaces, some of them marshy, some of them dry; some filled with shrubs and young trees, some mostly bare apart from the flower-rich pasture. We hear the call of a cuckoo somewhere – my first of the year. Ted keeps his eyes firmly on the ground. He's searching for signs that soil fungi are flourishing below ground in the way the birds and butterflies are above ground. He's looking for fruiting bodies – mushrooms to you and me.

We find plenty of them. After the scorched-earth practices of intensive agriculture when the fungal life of the soil would have been marginal, these key drivers of mature ecosystems are coming back in a big way. Ted explains how they work.

There are the species that can be collectively called 'recyclers'. In the soil these fungi are the main agents of decay. They release enzymes that can break down some of the most durable substances in nature – the fibrous lignin and cellulose of plants; the hard, chitin shells of insects; even animal bones. The nutrients released by the breakdown of these materials are absorbed by the recyclers through their cell walls. Most are later released along with enzymes and wastes left behind as the fungus continues to grow. These compounds are then available for bacteria to break down, freeing them for use by plants or other soil organisms.

Then there's a second group of soil fungi, referred to by Ted as 'food gatherers'. These are the mycorrhizal fungi, which, as we have seen, work in close partnership with living plants. Ted is particularly interested in the group of mycorrhizal fungi known as 'ectomycorrhizal' fungi. These are mostly associated with trees, both hardwoods and conifers. They grow close to the surface of tree roots, sometimes even forming webs or protective 'gloves' around them. They are, says Ted, the plant's first line of defence against pathogens trying to enter their roots.

But such is the damage done to soil fungi – and other beneficial organisms – by fertilisers, pesticides and the rest, Britain's trees are under greater disease attack than ever before. Ted has a stark warning about human health, too. Soil fungi could also be protecting human health but our profligate use of chemicals in farming has robbed us of this protection.

Grasses, vegetables and shrubs are linked to a second group of mycorrhizal fungi known as 'endomycorrhizae'. These don't simply enclose plant roots in a protective sheath. They actually penetrate the plant's root cells, taking the carbohydrates they need from the plant and using the energy to extend out into the soil. In effect they extend the plant's root system, growing into crevices the roots couldn't access and passing back moisture and nutrients.

Mycorrhizal fungi don't work in isolation. They form intricate networks in the soil, often carrying water and nutrients to a number of different plants. Many plants depend on them for a supply of the element phosphorus. They produce acids that can release chemically-bound phosphorus in the soil and make it available for host plants. They also free up other essential elements such as copper, calcium, magnesium, zinc and iron.

Commercial crops and vegetables are so heavily dosed with chemical fertilisers that mycorrhizae are severely depleted on modern farmland. The same applies to most agricultural grasslands, which are generally monocultures of a single grass variety heavily dosed with artificial fertiliser. In the wildlands of Knepp Estate, cattle and deer eat vegetation that is protected by fully functioning mycorrhizae. Not only are they able to select the foods they need, those foods are full of nutrients thanks to a fertile, biologically-active soil. Which means that when the animals are sold for meat, consumers are getting a product with the full nutrient package that human hunter-gatherers would have benefited from before the invention of agriculture and the slow degradation of our foods.

Charlie Burrell sells his beef to Garlic Wood Farm, which specialises in the meat of animals grazing species-rich pastures, many of them on nature reserves. But at the moment the market won't return a price that reflects the true value of what must surely be 'super meats'. Not surprisingly, Charlie thinks it's time we all took a long, hard look at the way our meat is produced. Does it make sense to cover our best farmland with cereals – with all the environmental damage this causes – only to feed half of them to animals?

As we stand listening to birdsong in a 'scrub' field of self-sown sallow, Charlie tells me of the reaction of some of his first cattle to modern, industrial grassland. He'd bought in some native English Longhorn cattle because he thought they'd be well suited to the wildland system. They very quickly found a field sown with modern Italian ryegrass, a leftover from when the land was farmed intensively. For half an hour the cattle gorged on these sweet-tasting, highly-bred grasses, an experience they hadn't had before.

Unfortunately they very quickly experienced digestive upsets, getting a bad attack of 'the runs'. They soon left the industrial pasture and went in search of something more wholesome. For the next month they hardly strayed from a wet field dominated by a coarse, fibrous plant known as barley grass. Once their digestive systems had settled down they never went near the 'fast-food' pasture again. Unlike humans, farm animals know instinctively the foods they need to stay healthy. Sadly, modern farming forces them to eat the kind of nutrient-depleted rubbish we do.

A photograph of Knepp's ginger pigs provided the perfect illustration. Ecologically their function is to do what pigs do best – to rootle around in pastures, turning it over in their search for worms and insects, in the process opening up new niches for vegetation. Early on in the experiment they were in a couple of fields that had recently come out of intensive arable cropping. The only part of those fields they were interested in was the line of a former footpath, the one area that had never been ploughed or sprayed with pesticides.

Charlie took a picture of a group of pigs lined up along the former footpath, rootling for worms and insects. Presumably they knew the former cropping area to be so devoid of life it wasn't worth bothering with. His picture of the footpath-following pigs went around the world, a clear demonstration of how intensive agriculture was wrecking the biodiversity of our soils. Like the truffle-seeking pigs of France, these English Tamworths were showing us something that could enrich our lives if we would only take notice of it.

Charlie recalls the visit of a group of farmers and landowners to the Knepp Estate project. The view of most of them was that he was 'putting the clock back'; returning to an older, failed system of agriculture. One outspoken member of the party described the project as 'immoral'. It was the farmer's duty to strive for maximum production to feed the world's hungry; in other words to grow high-input grain crops from boundary to boundary. Yet this is the system that has clearly failed.

What Charlie Burrell has done at Knepp is recreate a landscape for producing food – or rather, he has allowed grazing and rootling animals to recreate it. The proponents of chemical wheat-growing present us with a stark choice. We can have wildlife or we can have food, they say. We can't have both. Hence the widespread view in farming that to opt for anything less than full-on production – with all the chemical fertilisers and pesticides – is a betrayal of the world's hungry.

The Knepp experiment shows that biodiversity is what makes a real food system work. Soils, with their vast living populations of bacteria, fungi, protozoa, millipedes, springtails and earthworms, are the source of life, whether for growing food crops or for sustaining wildlife populations. It's no coincidence that crop yields are falling at a time when Britain's wildlife is under pressure. The cause is the same: soil destruction by a faulty view of food production.

A team of researchers from Bournemouth University looked at two different approaches to maintaining biodiversity – by maintaining a number of small, separate wildlife sites, as now, or by creating big, landscape-scale projects as at Knepp. The researchers assessed the two approaches through their success in delivering 'ecosystem services', a catch-all phrase for a whole range of environmental benefits. They found that the landscape approach not only produced food, it also delivered raw materials and fibre, flood protection, energy and fuel, recreation and carbon storage. The combined value of these extra 'services' was worth many times more than the food alone. Surely another reason for rolling out real food landscapes across a greater area of Britain?

Despite what the apologists for intensive agriculture would have us believe, a flourishing wildlife population is not a distraction from the business of producing food. It doesn't mean our priorities are wrong. Quite the opposite. It's a sign that we're getting it right. It's the mark of a healthy landscape, a healthy soil and a healthy environment. And it's the best guarantee we have that we can stay healthy too.

The experiment at Knepp provides vital clues, not only to the way our farming has gone wrong, but to the way we could do things better in the future. As a direct model for food production it may have its limitations. Realistically it's not likely to produce enough, at least for the kind of meat-rich diets many of us choose at the moment. Charlie Burrell reports that the rewilded estate produced 36 tonnes of meat in 2015, worth £120,000.

As the system matures it may turn out to be far more productive. When soil biology is really ramped up there seems almost no limit to what the land will produce. But for the moment this rewilded landscape can't be seen as a viable farming system. It may produce the healthiest meats imaginable, packed with the sorts of nutrients evolution has adapted us for. But if there isn't enough of the stuff, the system is of limited value. What it can do, however, is show us how we could change our present methods to make our foods more nutritious and our agriculture more sustainable.

At Knepp our countryside has effectively been reset to its default 'factory setting'. This is not unlike the forest home of our hunter-gatherer forebears. If we were inventing agriculture afresh, could we do it differently this time around? Could we retain the rich diversity of this ecosystem while subtly tweaking it to produce more of the foods we need?

In nutrient terms the meat from this profusion of foliage and fertile soil must be worth far more than the grain-fed meats we eat today. So we can safely eat less meat while being better nourished. But could we also grow our vegetables on these soils so rich in biodiversity? Could we grow our vegetables, fruits and whatever cereal grains we need in this forest setting? Perhaps there could be temporary plots for cultivation over a year or two, producing the kind of nutrient-rich foods that nourished our pre-farming ancestors.

Imagine the green belts around our towns and cities providing these kinds of foods, while at the same time cleaning up our rivers, sucking carbon from the atmosphere and protecting residential areas from flooding. It's a beguiling idea. Far from creating many of our major challenges, farming could at last become what it surely should be, the solution.

But that's for the future. It's now time to investigate how we as individuals can source the foods we need in today's less-than-perfect world. Is there a real possibility of eating like our ancestors in a world dominated by Big Wheat and other agribusiness hoaxes?

CHAPTER 10

Our grass-fed future

It's hard not to feel disconsolate about the prospects for real foods returning any time soon, at least on a large scale. Much of our best farmland remains locked in the toxic embrace of industrial agriculture. The subsidy mindset that underpins it appears as immutable as ever. Any threat to the public handouts brings militant farmers out onto the streets and has UK farmers' unions muttering darkly about the end of agriculture as we know it.

It would be difficult to overstate the damage done by farm subsidies to our food supply. They have stifled initiative and deadened the entrepreneurial spirit for generations of farmers. Instead they've kept them shackled to a production system that benefits no one but the pesticide companies and the big food processors.

Without the state handouts it's likely that farmers would have been leading the campaign for real food. They'd be out banging the drum on behalf of the naturally-grown foods of the countryside. Thanks to state interference they've become commodity slaves for the food corporations. Has there ever been a dependency culture so damaging to the public interest as the publicly-funded farm subsidies?

As I said, it's easy to feel gloomy. But actually I'm not.

I'm very optimistic about the future of food and farming in Britain. Odd though it may seem, the signs of hope are mainly to be seen in the United States. The home of the most grotesque animal factories on the planet is witnessing an incredible grass-fed food movement.

Unlike British people, most Americans now know the significance of the term 'grass-fed'. A growing number of them – appalled by the feedlot practices of routine antibiotic and growth hormone use – have taken to buying grass-fed meat direct from the farm.

A Google of 'grass-fed meat' produces many millions of sites, the great majority of them in the US. For beef alone the retail value of grass-fed has gone from around $5 million in 1998 to over $400 million in 2013. In the decade before, the market had grown by 25 to 30 per cent annually.[1]

With the exception of Whole Foods Market, the major US food retailers have been largely excluded from this new food phenomenon. Customers are going direct to farmers, buying frozen meat by mail order or at farm shops and farmers' markets.

In American cities, grass-fed restaurants and burger bars are springing up like mushrooms in an old meadow. Whether it's a prime steak or a burger, a growing number of Americans want to be sure it's from cattle grazing on fresh pastures, rich in clovers and herbs, and to which little or no chemical fertiliser has been applied.

It's a movement that's bringing new prosperity to rural areas. Feedlots still dominate US meat production, of course, and the nation's crop lands are still mostly occupied by pesticide-ridden monocultures. But grass-fed foods are breaking the stranglehold of large corporations on food production. Farmers large and small are discovering that supplying real foods direct to consumers can pay handsomely.

Demand for grass-fed foods is ending farmers' enslavement to big agribusiness. No longer are they reliant on chemical companies, fertiliser companies, machinery dealers, diesel fuel suppliers and the banks who finance it all. They are producing natural products, foods from animals grazing naturally on herb-rich pastures, the foods nature intended us to eat.

Ranchers across America are now opting, not to put their young cattle into feedlots for fattening, but to finish them on pasture. They are returning to the production patterns of the cowboys in the old West. Back east, small farmers who have been marginalised in the rush to big-scale commodity production now find that in grass-fed foods they have products they can sell online across America – for good prices.

The shift to grass-fed doesn't mean a shift to low-output agriculture. Many of the most successful grass-fed food producers are highly intensive. But it's an intensity not built on chemicals. It's an intensity that's principally biological.

Many of the new grazers practise enterprise 'stacking', which means running a variety of animal and bird species on their pastures. Poultry and pigs can be 'pastured' in a similar way to ruminants like cattle, sheep, goats and deer. The non-ruminant species need additional grain feeds, but running them on grass allows them to obtain a lot of their nutrients from plants and insects. This makes the meat and eggs better-tasting while giving the foods a healthier range of nutrients.

Mixing up the species is a natural way of utilising grasslands. In the wild all these species would be sharing the same space. If it's managed well on the farm it can build soil fertility and restore carbon to impoverished soil.

Some of the most successful American grassland farmers are selling a wide range of foods from their farm shops and online stores. Grass-fed beef, lamb, milk, butter and cheese are stocked alongside pastured eggs, pastured pork, pastured goose and pastured duck. Some farms even list cosmetic items such as body butter, soaps and lip balm, all made from grass-fed or pastured animal products.[2]

Grass-fed real foods are bringing about a revolution in rural America. This kind of natural farming is known as 'regenerative agriculture' principally because of the way it restores damaged soils to health and fertility. But it also regenerates farm businesses, rural communities and wildlife-rich countryside.

All this is happening on the other side of the Atlantic. By comparison, change in Britain has been slow but is now gaining momentum. It's driven mainly by the Paleo movement, the natural eating programme devised by Loren Cordain, and also known as the 'caveman diet'. The market is catered for by such websites as Primal Meats, Paleo Nutrition Wales and Athleat. Another 'entry point' to grass-fed foods is through the popular fitness programme known as CrossFit, which was developed in the US.

I talked to a former Royal Marine officer who had been introduced to grass-fed foods through the CrossFit programme. In earlier life he'd been a keen rugby player and at that time believed high-carbohydrate foods to be the way to improve performance. But on a tour of duty in Iraq he met members of US Special Forces who were working out using CrossFit. In conversation with them he discovered the Paleo diet and the health advantages of grass-fed meat.

Years later, and on becoming a father, his dietary choices moved beyond the strictly Paleo approach, which rules out post-agricultural foods such as wheat and dairy products. The ex-Marine told me he now enjoyed dairy foods such as milk, butter, cream and cheese. But they all needed to come from cows grazing clover-rich pasture and fed little or no grain. The milk also had to be raw and unpasteurised.

Farmer Will Buckley raises grass-fed beef and lamb, as well as pastured pork, on flower-filled pastures in the Test Valley in Hampshire. He's also opened Britain's first grass-fed food restaurant in a busy street close to Southampton city centre. Called Chalk Valley Farm and Kitchen, it's what's known in the US as a 'farm-to-table' restaurant.

On the menu are a wide range of dishes using grass-fed beef, buffalo and lamb, along with pastured pork and chicken. There's also a delicious range of salads. Will Buckley says his core clientele are currently fitness enthusiasts, particularly those who have adopted the CrossFit programme. All are knowledgeable on the benefits of the Paleo diet.

I chatted to Will about his plans for the future as we strolled around his farm near Stockbridge. In the summer sunshine his beautiful Devon cattle – known in the West Country as Red Rubies – were quietly grazing in river meadows containing legumes such as clover and vetch along with deep-rooting herbs like chicory and plantain.

Will has an ambition to open a series of restaurants across Britain. But for that to happen the health benefits of grass-fed and pastured foods will need to be understood by a far wider section of the public than the fitness community. In the US this has happened, but in Britain it may take longer for the message to get out there.

The irony is that a couple of generations ago most of us in Britain ate grass-fed foods. This was the default production system. It's the practice of feeding grain that's new.

Today, finding grass-fed foods can be a matter of sheer luck. Once a week Simon Cutter drives a refrigerated delivery van from his farm in Herefordshire to the Bearwood district of Birmingham. On board he carries a wide selection of seasonal vegetables, organic eggs, fruit juice and locally-produced milk and dairy foods, including a range of unpasteurised cheeses.

But by far the biggest part of the load is made up of meat from the animals that graze on or range over his herb-filled pastures. They include beef and lamb, mutton and poultry meat, all cut up, packed and labelled in his own farm shop. There are cuts of free-range pork along with sausages and burgers. There's even a selection of free-range 'wild things' such as diced venison, venison steaks and rabbit meat. What it adds up to is a van-load of the authentic foods and flavours from a countryside that isn't subject to the chemical battering inflicted on most farms today. They're destined for a group of discriminating consumers who appreciate foods like these.

Bearwood Pantry was set up a few years ago by a group of young mums who wanted something better for their children than the foods on offer in their local high street. What they were after were naturally-grown foods, rich in health-protecting nutrients and produced at nature's own pace.

These weren't the kinds of foods they could find in their local supermarkets, not even the up-market sort. Things weren't any better in the independent food shops. The food-savvy women investigated independent butchers' shops in the hope of finding organic meat, surely not too much to expect on a busy high street in Britain's second city. Sadly it was.

One of Bearwood Pantry's founder members, Cathryn (Kate) Bevan, recalls: 'The butchers told us they didn't really do organic. There wasn't much of a market for it. It seems that in our part of the city at least, the best foods were simply not available.'

Fortunately one of Kate's friends knew of Simon Cutter, who with his two sons runs Model Farm at Hildersley, near Ross-on-Wye. It was a chance recommendation that led to the Bearwood group entering into a long-term relationship with the farm. It means they now enjoy the very best foods at prices to match those of 'ordinary' foods in the supermarket.

Simon Cutter knows a thing or two about producing good foods. He's a supplier-member of the Pasture-Fed Livestock Association, whose rules stipulate that ruminant animals such as cattle and sheep are fed no cereal grains at any point in their life-cycle. This means the meats they produce are better than organic. They feed only on pastures rich in clovers and herbs, or on conserved hay or silage made from those same species-rich pastures. The result is superb meat, rich in vitamin E, omega-3 fatty acids and the anti-cancer compound CLA.

One bright autumn day I took a stroll around Model Farm. My guide, Simon, told me it was originally established as one of a cluster of small farms provided by the local authority for soldiers returning from the Crimean War. Though the land isn't particularly good, the farm is now highly fertile. Educated in farming at Cirencester's Royal Agricultural University, Simon has been studying and practising traditional farming for more than twenty years. He has clearly refined it to a very high standard.

Like the best farms producing high-quality food, the whole place is bursting with life. The flower-filled pastures are alive with insects and butterflies, while the hedges and treetops ring with birdsong. In addition there are soil-enriching crops of lucerne, vetches and red clover.

Into this symphony of life the mostly native-breed livestock blend naturally and easily. They include Hereford cattle, 'easy-care' sheep and beautiful black-and-white Hampshire pigs, an American breed that Simon describes as 'Saddleback-like, but with ears that stick up rather than flop down'. All the animals are free-range, growing at their own pace in their own natural setting. It's a system designed to produce the tastiest, healthiest animal foods possible. And once a week Simon takes a sample of these great foods to town.

The Birmingham families who buy food through Bearwood Pantry place their orders online during the week. Most of the foods come from Model Farm and a handful of associated farms working with the Cutter family. The foods are packed and labelled in the farm shop, then delivered to a central drop-off point on Thursday afternoon.

Later, members call to collect their food. With each order there's an invoice from Model Farm. Members pay on the night by cash, cheque or debit card. Bearwood Pantry organisers say no one is pressured to buy or to make any long-term commitment. Having joined the group they are free to use the service whenever they choose.

Food groups like Bearwood Pantry could be set up anywhere in Britain – in city centres, in leafy suburbs and in rural areas. It's a way for community groups to connect with a living countryside and a vibrant soil life. There's the chance to buy nutrient-rich foods at the same prices as the dumbed-down versions in supermarkets. Because farmers are selling direct, they, too, can make a decent living, allowing them to farm in the humane, environmentally-friendly way.

One of the new players in Britain's embryonic grass-fed movement is farmer Ollie White, who runs Farm2Fork from a small rented farm near Ilminster in Somerset. His website outlines the basics of the Paleo diet. There's also a summary of the health benefits of grass-fed meat.

He currently sells his own grass-fed beef and lamb through a box scheme run from the farm. The lamb is from his flock of Poll Dorset sheep, which graze all year round on pastures rich in grasses, herbs and legumes. The beef cattle are all native breeds – Aberdeen Angus, Hereford and Devon. They, too, graze herb-rich pastures. Ollie explains that he buys the cattle in as 'stores', animals that are not yet ready for market. Then they're finished on pastures alone. It means they're 100 per cent grass-fed and grass-finished, he says.

Farm2Fork also runs a flourishing Christmas geese enterprise. The geese, like the cattle and sheep, run on the herb-rich pastures.

For Ollie the developing market for grass-fed foods offers an unprecedented opportunity for small farmers like him to build successful businesses. The internet plus the rise of social media means they can take their message of health and sound nutrition to consumers in a way that would have been unimaginable a decade ago. He's convinced that in Britain the growth of grass-fed foods will be 'farmer driven'. Their businesses will grow only as quickly as they can take the true story of livestock and grazing to a wider audience. That's why he believes time spent honing his social media skills is as valuable as that spent running the farm.

Can farmers like Ollie White with their animals and flower-filled grasslands bring about a food and farming revolution in Britain? That rather depends on us, the nation's consumers. Our politicians have shown little appetite for taking on the food manufacturers and agribusiness interests, who between them keep the present disastrous system in place.

The major food retailers would be in a strong position to change things if they wanted to. But so far they've shown little interest in grass-fed food, presumably because it would challenge so many of their existing brands. Supermarkets offer a fantastic choice, so long as it's not real food you're after.

I've spent a lot of time in my local supermarkets looking for grass-fed foods. Sadly they're rarely to be found. To be fair, most of the British lamb they sell in summer and autumn is probably grass-fed. And there might be the odd speciality cheese from the French Alps. But there's no way of being sure because they're not labelled.

As for beef, most British cattle spend part of their lives grazing fresh pasture or munching on preserved grass in the form of silage. But during the final weeks of the production process they're likely to be fed grain, so many of the nutritional benefits of grazing are lost. Organic cattle are guaranteed to get a good part of their feed in the form of grazed pasture or silage. But they too can be fed grain – albeit organic grain – during the crucial finishing period.

Supermarket milk – as we've seen – is a disaster area. Most of it is so highly processed it bears little resemblance to the real thing. Some heavily processed milks are now being 'enriched' with added vitamins and minerals, presumably to replace the ones lost because of the farming and processing methods used in their production. Even organic milk is likely to have come from cows fed large amounts of grain, so many of the health benefits will have been lost or diluted.

Despite the lack of interest of retailers, it shouldn't be difficult to find grass-fed foods. They're out there if we care to look. It's worth remembering that we're hunter-gatherers. It's time to go out and gather. Even if the full Paleo diet isn't for us, it's worth making sure the meat and dairy foods we eat are the real thing.

I've managed to find grass-fed beef at my local farmers' market. It's produced by a middle-aged couple who love their small farm so much they want to take care of it, which means keeping grazing animals. Their Aberdeen Angus beef is not certified by any official body. But I've got to know them well enough to be confident that for the crucial months of finishing their animals feed on pasture alone.

If there were no local producer I'd look online for the right kinds of food. The first site to visit is the PFLA, the Pasture-Fed Livestock Association, whose certified producers guarantee that no grain has been fed for the animal's lifetime. But whether your chosen supplier is a PFLA member or not, it's worth visiting the farm if you can. After all, no one else you do business with will have as great an effect on your well-being as the farm supplying your food.

When you buy food direct from a farmer like this you're entering into a joint venture to make our country better. Your main concern is to buy good food, of course. But when it's grass-fed food you'll also be helping to restore the fertility of our farmland as well as increasing the numbers of our wildlife. You'll be putting money directly into the local economy, where it'll support village post offices and shops, pubs and other rural businesses. When you buy food from the major retailers you're simply enriching City investors.

The grass-fed movement is for people. It's an alliance between those who grow our food and those who choose to eat something better than big business offers us. Without wishing to sound like a dangerous revolutionary, it's about giving power back to people; that most basic power, the power to reclaim the foods evolution prepared us for. At its heart it's all about democracy.

Further Reading

E.B. Balfour, *The Living Soil*, Faber & Faber, 1943, new edition from Soil Association, 2006

Richard Bardgett, *The Biology of Soil: A Community and Ecosystem Approach*, Oxford University Press, 2005

Wendell Berry, *The Gift of Gravity: Selected Poems 1968–2000*, Golgonooza Press, 2002

Martin Blaser, *Missing Microbes*, Oneworld Publications, 2014

Richard Body, *Agriculture: The Triumph and the Shame*, Temple-Smith, 1982

J.K. Bowers and Paul Cheshire, *Agriculture, the Countryside and Land Use: An Economic Critique*, Methuen, 1983

Jerry Brunetti, *The Farm as Ecosystem: Tapping Nature's Reservoir*, Acres USA, 2014

Natasha Campbell-McBride, *Put Your Heart in Your Mouth*, Medinform, 2007

Natasha Campbell-McBride, *Gut and Psychology Syndrome*, Medinform, 2010

Surgeon Captain T.L. Cleave, *The Saccharine Disease*, John Wright, 1974

Loren Cordain, *The Paleo Diet*, revised edition, John Wiley, 2011

Steven M. Druker, *Altered Genes, Twisted Truth: How the Venture to Genetically Engineer Our Food Has Subverted Science, Corrupted Government, and Systematically Deceived the Public*, Clear River Press, 2015

Robert H. Elliot, *The Clifton Park System of Farming*, Faber & Faber, 1898

Sally Fallon, *Nourishing Traditions*, New Trends Publishing, 2001

Masanobu Fukuoka, *The One-Straw Revolution*, Other India Press, 1992

Zoe Harcombe, *The Obesity Epidemic*, Columbus Publishing, 2010

George Henderson, *The Farming Ladder*, Faber & Faber, 1944

Arthur Hollins, *The Farmer, the Plough and the Devil: The Story of Fordhall Farm*, Ashgrove Press, 1984

Sir Albert Howard, *An Agricultural Testament*, Other India Press, 1943; the full text is now online at: journeytoforever.com

Malcolm Kendrick, *The Great Cholesterol Con: The Truth About What Really Causes Heart Disease and How to Avoid It,* John Blake, 2008

James Le Fanu, *The Rise and Fall of Modern Medicine*, Little Brown, 1999

Daniel E. Lieberman, *The Story of the Human Body: Evolution, Health and Disease*, Vintage, 2014

Jeff Lowenfels and Wayne Lewis, *Teeming With Microbes: The Organic Gardener's Guide to the Soil Food Web*, Timber Press, 2013

Max B. Lurie, *Resistance to Tuberculosis: Experimental Studies in Native and Acquired Defensive Mechanisms*, Harvard University Press, 1964

Philip Lymbery with Isabel Oakeshott, *Farmageddon: The True cost of Cheap Meat*, Bloomsbury, 2014

Charles C. Mann, *1491: New Revelations of the Americas Before Columbus*, Knopf, 2005
Richard Manning, *Grassland: The History, Biology, Politics and Promise of the American Prairie*, Penguin Books USA, 1995
H.J. Massingham, *The Wisdom of the Fields*, Collins, 1945

Ames B. Nardi, *Life in the Soil: A Guide for Naturalists and Gardeners*, University of Chicago Press, 2007
Frank Newman Turner, *Fertility Pastures*, Faber & Faber, 1950
Frank Newman Turner, *Fertility Farming*, Faber & Faber, 1951

Michael Pollan, *The Omnivore's Dilemma: The Search for a Perfect Meal in a Fast-Food World*, Bloomsbury, 2006
Jules Pretty, *The Living Land: Agriculture, Food and Community Regeneration in Rural Europe*, Earthscan, 1998
Weston A. Price, *Nutrition and Physical Degeneration*, sixth edition, Price-Pottenger Nutrition Foundation, 2004

Oliver Rackham, *The History of the Countryside*, Weidenfeld & Nicolson, London, 1995
Jo Robinson, *Why Grassfed is Best*, Vashon Island Press, Vashon, Washington, 2000

Ron Schmid, *The Untold Story of Milk*, New Trends Publishing, 2003
E.F. Schumacher, *Small is Beautiful. A Study of Economics as if People Mattered*, Blond and Briggs, 1973
Judith D. Schwartz, *Cows Save the Planet: And Other Improbable Ways of Restoring Soil to Heal the Earth*, Chelsea Green Publishing, 2013

Marion Shoard, *The Theft of the Countryside*, Temple-Smith, 1980
Sir George Stapledon, *The Way of the Land*, Faber & Faber, 1943
Chris Stringer, *Homo Britannicus: The Incredible Story of Human Life in Britain*, Penguin Books, 2006

Gary Taubes, *The Diet Delusion*, Vermilion, 2008

André Voisin, *Grass Productivity*, Crosby Lockwood, 1959
André Voisin, *Soil, Grass and Cancer: The Link Between Human and Animal Health and the Mineral Balance of the Soil*, Philosophical Library, 1959, new edition from Acres USA, 1999

Norman Wirzba (ed.), *The Essential Agrarian Reader: The Future of Culture, Community and the Land*, University Press of Kentucky, 2003

Walter W. Yellowlees, *A Doctor in the Wilderness*, Janus Publishing Company, 1993

Notes

Introduction

1. David Wembridge, *The state of Britain's hedgehogs 2011*, British Hedgehog Preservation Society/People's Trust for Endangered Species; www.britishhedgehogs.org.uk/leaflets/sobh.pdf.

Chapter 1: Darwin's diet

1. 'Study reveals sharp rise in people at risk of getting diabetes', *The Guardian*, 10 June 2014. Taken from BMJ Open.
2. A.S. Ahmad, N. Ormiston-Smith and P.D. Sasieni, 'Trends in the lifetime risk of developing cancer in Great Britain: comparison of risk for those born from 1930 to 1960', *British Journal of Cancer*, 2015.
3. David Pimental and Michael Burgess, *Agriculture* 2013, 3, pp. 443–63; doi:10.3390/agriculture/3030443.
4. World Health Organization, *Nutrition for Health and Development: A Global Agenda for Combating Malnutrition; Progress Report*, WHO, Nutrition for Health and Development (NHD), Sustainable Development and Healthy Environments (SDE), Rome, Italy, 2000. Online at: whqlibdoc.who.int/hq/2000/WHO_NHD_00.6.pdf.
5. David Pimental, 'Soil Erosion: A food and environmental threat', *Environment, Development and Sustainability*, 2006, 8, pp. 119–37.
6. Gary Taubes, *The Diet Delusion*, Vermilion, 2008, pp. 89–99.
7. Ibid., pp. 91–3.

8. *Open Heart*, 2015; 2: doi: 10.1136/openhrt-2014-000196corr1.
9. Jared Diamond, 'The worst mistake in the history of the human race', *Discover Magazine*, May 1987, pp. 64–6.
10. K. Milton, 'Nutritional characteristics of wild primate foods: Do the diets of our closest living relatives have lessons for us?', *Nutrition* 15, 1999, pp. 488–98; S.B. Eaton, S.B. Eaton III, and M.J. Konner, 'Paleolithic nutrition revisited: A twelve-year retrospective on its nature and implications', *European Journal of Clinical Nutrition*, 51, 1997, pp. 207–16.
11. Habiba Chirchir, et al., 'Recent origin of low trabecular bone density in modern humans', *Proceedings of the US National Academy of Sciences*, 2015, vol. 112, No. 2, pp. 366–71.
12. Daniel E. Lieberman, *The Story of the Human Body: Evolution, Health and Disease*, Vintage, 2014, pp. 235–6.
13. Ibid.
14. Andrew Stringer, *The Food Fallacy*, MME&T Publications, 2008, p. 47.
15. Loren Cordain, *The Paleo Diet*, revised edition, John Wiley, 2011, p. 25.
16. Zoe Harcombe, *The Obesity Epidemic*, Columbus Publishing, 2010, p. 151; www.theobesityepidemic.org.
17. Michael Gurven and Hillard Kaplan, 'Longevity among hunter-gatherers: A cross-cultural examination', www.anth.ucsb.edu/faculty/gurven/papers/GurvenKaplan2007pdr.pdf.
18. Weston A. Price, *Nutrition and Physical Degeneration*, sixth edition, Price-Pottenger Nutrition Foundation, 2004.
19. Natasha Campbell-McBride, *Gut and Psychology Syndrome*, Medinform, 2010.
20. Natasha Campbell-McBride, *Put Your Heart in Your Mouth*, Medinform, 2007.

Chapter 2: How grass makes you healthy

1. Susan Allport, 'The Queen of Fats: An Author's Quest to Restore Omega-3 to the Western Diet', *Acres USA*, April 2008, pp. 56–62; www.susanallport.com.
2. M. Studer, et al., 'Effect of different antilipidemic agents and diets on mortality', *Archives of Internal Medicine*, 165, 2005, pp. 725–30.
3. C.M. Benbrook, et al., 'Organic Production Enhances Milk Nutritional Quality by Shifting Fatty Acid Composition: A United States-Wide, 18-Month Study', PLoS ONE, 2013, 8(12).
4. F.M. Whittington and J.D. Wood, 'Effect of Pasture Type on Lamb Product Quality', from *Eating Biodiversity: An Investigation of the Links Between Quality Food Production and Biodiversity Protection*, a report from Bristol University, 2006.
5. T.R. Dhiman, et al., 'Conjugated Linoleic Acid Content of Milk From Cows Fed Different Diets', *Journal of Dairy Science*, 1999, vol. 82 (10), pp. 2146–56.
6. H. Timmen and S. Patton, 'Milk Fat Globules: Fatty Acid Composition, Size and In Vivo Regulation of Fat Liquidity', *Lipids*, 1988, vol. 23, pp. 685–9.
7. C. Edgar Sheaffer, 'Grass Gives Life', *Acres USA*, May 2007, pp. 78–9.
8. D. McDonagh, et al., 'Milk and Dairy Products for Better Human Health', Teagasc – Irish Agricultural and Food Development Authority; www.teagasc.ie.
9. Jo Robinson, *Why Grassfed is Best*, Vashon Island Press, Vashon, Washington, 2000, p. 22.
10. Marius Collomb, et al., 'Correlation Between Fatty Acids in Cows' Milk Produced in Lowlands, Mountains and Highlands of Switzerland and Botanical Composition of Fodder', *International Dairy Journal*, 2002, vol. 12, pp. 661–8.

11. C.A. Daley, et al., 'A Literature Review of the Value Added Nutrients Found in Grass-fed Beef Products', *Nutrition Journal*, June 2006.
12. Gonzales Diez, et al., 'Grain Feeding and the Dissemination of Acid Resistant *Eschericia coli* from Cattle', *Science*, 1998, vol. 281, pp. 1666–8.

Chapter 3: Our occupied land

1. Richard Young, 'The fat of the land: Eating red meat', Sustainable Food Trust, 13 June 2014; sustainablefoodtrust.org/articles/redmeat.
2. James Le Fanu, *The Rise and Fall of Modern Medicine*, Little Brown, 1999, pp. 210–15.
3. Zoe Harcombe, 2010, op. cit., p. 280.
4. Gary Taubes, 2008, op. cit., p. 113.
5. Ibid., pp. 451–2.
6. Ibid., p. 454.
7. Daniel E. Lieberman, 2014, op. cit., pp. 266–7.
8. Bethanie Afton, 'A lesson in Victorian sustainable agriculture: Husbandlike farming on the chalklands of Hampshire', *Research Series Number 2*, 1997, University of Reading Rural History Centre.
9. Environment Agency, *The State of Soils in England and Wales*, 2004.
10. Environment Agency, *The Total External Environmental Costs and Benefits of Agriculture in the UK*, 2007.
11. Luca Montanarella, 'Soil at the interface between agriculture and environment', *Agriculture and Environment*, The European Commission; ec.europa.eu/agriculture/envir/report/en/inter_en/report.htm.

12. Noah Fierer, et al., 'Reconstructing the Microbial Diversity and Function of Pre-Agricultural Tallgrass Prairie Soils in the United States', *Science*, 1 November 2013, pp. 621–4.
13. Mary C. Scholes, Robert J. Scholes, 'Dust Unto Dust', *Science*, 1 November 2013, pp. 565–6.
14. Andro Linklater, *Owning the Earth*, Bloomsbury, 2013, p. 341.
15. 'Pesticide Residues in Food', Annual Report 2011, PRiF.
16. 'Pesticides on a Plate', Pesticide Action Network, 2013; www.pan-uk.org.
17. www.pesticide.org/get-the-facts/pesticide-factsheets/glyphosate.
18. Anthony Samsel, Stephanie Seneff, 'Glyphosate's Suppression of Cytochrome P450 Enzymes and Amino Acid Biosynthesis by the Gut Microbiome: Pathways to Modern Diseases', *Entropy*, 2013, 15, pp. 1416–63.
19. UK Agriculture; www.ukagriculture.com.
20. K.C. Tyson, et al., 'Comparison of Crop Yields and Soil Conditions During 30 Years Under Annual Tillage or Grazed Pasture', *Journal of Agricultural Science*, vol. 115, 1990, pp. 29–40.

Chapter 4: A landscape for life

1. Oliver Rackham, *The History of the Countryside*, Weidenfeld & Nicolson, London, 1995.
2. *Agriculture at a Crossroads*, International Assessment of Agricultural Knowledge, Science and Technology for Development, 2008; www.unep.org/dewa/agassessment/reports/IAASTD/EN/Agriculture%20at%20a%20Crossroads_Synthesis%20Report%20(English).pdf.
3. George Stapledon, 'The Reclamation of Grasslands', in *England and the Farmer*, ed. H.J. Massingham, Batsford, 1941, p. 152.

4. Sir George Stapledon, *The Way of the Land*, Faber & Faber, 1943, p. 181.
5. Nigel D. Boatman, Hazel Parry, et al., 'Impacts of Agricultural Change on Farmland Biodiversity in the UK', in *Biodiversity Under Threat*, R.E. Hester and R.M. Harrison, eds, *Issues in Environmental Science and Technology*, No. 25, 2007, The Royal Society of Chemistry; Academia.edu/414709/Impacts_of_Agricultural_Change_on_Farmland_Biodiversity_in_the_UK.

Chapter 5: The dodgy science that steals our food

1. Elizabeth Truss, speech at the National Farmers' Union conference, 24 February 2015; Department for Environment, Food and Rural Affairs: www.gov.uk/government/speeches/elizabeth-truss-speech-at-national-farmers-union-conference.
2. *Agriculture in the United Kingdom 2014*, Department for Environment, Food and Rural Affairs, 2015, p. 91.
3. *A UK Strategy for Agricultural Technologies*, Industrial Strategy: government and industry in partnership, HM Government, July 2013.
4. 'Lincolnshire grower shatters world record for wheat yield', *Farmers Weekly*, 28 August 2015, pp. 50–51.
5. *Agriculture at a Crossroads*, 2008, op. cit.
6. 'Global farming expert challenges food crisis analysis', press release of the All Party Parliamentary Group on Agroecology, 11 March 2011.
7. 'GM science plea', *The Times*, 13 October 2011.
8. 'Use GM crops – or Britons may go unfed, says report', *The Guardian*, 14 March 2014.
9. 'Scientists' hidden links to the GM food giants', *Daily Mail*, 15 March 2014.

10. 'Bold new plans unveiled for a 20 per cent global yield boost', *Farmers Guardian*, 27 September 2013.
11. BASF advertisement, *Farmers Guardian*, 4 October 2013.
12. *Opportunity Agriculture: The next decade*, The Oxford Farming Conference, 2014, p. 78.
13. 'CPA blasts anti-science stance on GMs', *Farmers Weekly*, 23 March 2012.
14. Albert Howard, 'Soil Fertility', in *England and the Farmer*, ed. H.J. Massingham, Batsford, 1941, p. 50.
15. www.soilfoodweb.com.
16. Lynda Brown, 'The roots of your health: Elaine Ingham on the science of soil', Sustainable Food Trust, March 2015; sustainable foodtrust.org/articles/roots-health-elaine-ingham-science-soil/.
17. Robert Waller, *Prophet of the New Age*, Faber & Faber, 1962, pp. 274–8.
18. Steven M. Druker, *Altered Genes, Twisted Truth: How the Venture to Genetically Engineer Our Food Has Subverted Science, Corrupted Government, and Systematically Deceived the Public*, Clear River Press, 2015, p. 391.
19. John Reeves, *The Roots of Health*, 2003.

Chapter 6: The power of pasture

1. Bill Murphy, *Greener Pastures On Your Side of the Fence*, Arriba Publishing, Colchester, Vermont, 1987, pp. 195–6.
2. Chris Stringer, *Homo Britannicus: The Incredible Story of Human Life in Britain*, Penguin Books, 2006, p. 39.
3. Graham Harvey, *The Forgiveness of Nature*, Jonathan Cape, 2001, pp. 149–64.
4. D.B. Johnstone-Wallace and K. Kennedy, 'Grazing Management Practices and Their Relationship to the Behaviour and Grazing

Habits of Cattle', *Journal of Agricultural Science*, 1944, vol. 34, pp. 190–97.

5. William Davies, *The Grass Crop*, Spon, 1952, p. 258.
6. Frank Newman Turner, *Fertility Farming*, Faber & Faber, 1951, pp. 67–8.
7. André Voisin, *Better Grassland Sward*, Crosby Lockwood, 1960, pp. 150–2.
8. David Lance, *Beef and Lamb From Permanent Pasture on the Full-Time Organic Farm: A System for the 21st Century*, 2010. Obtainable from: David Lance, 117 Oaklands Park, Buckfastleigh, Devon, TQ11 0BW.
9. 'The Grassfed Primer', Animal Welfare Approved, 2015; animalwelfareapproved.org/wp-content/uploads/2015/09/The-Grassfed-Primer-AGW-2015-ONLINE.pdf.
10. Martin Blaser, *Missing Microbes*, Oneworld Publications, 2014, p. 82.
11. Ibid., p. 83.
12. Charles Darwin, *On the Origin of Species by Means of Natural Selection*, John Murray, 1859, p. 85.
13. www.pasturepromise.tv/graham-harvey-talks-to-joel-salatin.html.
14. Joel Salatin, 'Amazing Grazing', *Acres USA*, May 2007.
15. Quoted in Richard Manning, *Grassland: The History, Biology, Politics and Promise of the American Prairie*, Penguin Books USA, 1995, p. 84.

Chapter 7: Grazing animals – our planet's best friends

1. H. Steinfeld, et al., *Livestock's Long Shadow: Environmental Issues and Options*, Food and Agriculture Organization of the United Nations, 29 November 2006.

2. *Tackling Climate Change through Livestock: A global assessment of emissions and mitigation opportunities*, Food and Agriculture Organization of the United Nations, 2013.
3. Daniel E. Lieberman, 2014, op. cit., p. 281.
4. L. Cordain, et al., 'Fatty acid analysis of wild ruminant tissues: Evolutionary implications for reducing diet-related chronic disease', *European Journal of Clinical Nutrition*, 56, 2002, pp. 181–91.
5. Charles C. Mann, *1491: New Revelations of the Americas Before Columbus*, Knopf, 2005, p. 318.
6. P.F. Dunfield, 'The soil methane sink', in D.S. Reay, et al., eds, *Greenhouse Gas Sinks*, CAB Wallingford UK, 2007, pp. 152–70.
7. www.ted.com/talks/allan_savory_how_to_green_the_world_s_deserts_and_reverse_climate_change?language=en.
8. D.S. Powlson, et al., 'Soil carbon sequestration to mitigate climate change: A critical re-examination to identify the true and the false', *European Journal of Soil Science*, February 2011, 62, pp. 42–55.
9. 'Save Our Soils: An interview with Dr Christine Jones', *Acres USA*, March 2015, vol. 45, No. 3.
10. Christine Jones, 'Carbon that counts', www.amazingcarbon.com.
11. Sir Albert Howard, 'Soil Fertility', in *England and the Farmer*, ed. H.J. Massingham, London: Batsford, 1941, pp. 48–50.
12. *Agriculture at a Crossroads*, 2008, op. cit.
13. Robert H. Elliot, *The Clifton Park System of Farming*, Faber & Faber, 1898, p. 139.
14. 'Water and Climate Risks Facing US Corn Production', *Ceres Report*, June 2014; www.ceres.org/resources/reports/water-and-climate-risks-facing-u.s.-corn-production-how-companies-and-investors-can-cultivate-sustainability.

Chapter 8: In search of real milk

1. Charles Sanford Porter, *Milk Diet as a Remedy for Chronic Disease*, Long Beach, California, 1905.
2. J.R. Crewe, 'Raw Milk Cures Many Diseases', *Certified Milk Magazine*, January 1929, pp. 3–6.
3. T. Slots, et al., 'Potentials to differentiate milk composition by different feeding strategies', *Journal of Dairy Science*, 92: 2057–66; doi:10.3168/jds.2008-1392.
4. Jo Robinson, *Why Grassfed is Best*, Vashon Island Press, Vashon, Washington, 2000, p. 22.
5. T.R. Dhiman, et al., 'Conjugated Linoleic Acid Content of Milk From Cows Fed Different Diets', *Journal of Dairy Science*, 1999, vol. 82 (10), pp. 2146–56.
6. H. Timmen and S. Patton, 'Milk Fat Globules: Fatty Acid Composition, Size and In Vivo Regulation of Fat Liquidity', *Lipids*, 1988, vol. 23, pp. 685–9.
7. Marius Collomb, et al., 'Correlation Between Fatty Acids in Cows' Milk Produced in Lowlands, Mountains and Highlands of Switzerland and Botanical Composition of the Fodder', *International Dairy Journal*, 2002, vol. 12, pp. 661–8.
8. J. Robertson and C. Fanning, *Omega-3 Polyunsaturated Fatty Acids in Organic and Conventional Milk*, University of Aberdeen, 2004.
9. Jonathan Long, 'Effective Control Strategy Keeps Mastitis Bills Down', *Farmers Weekly*, 21 October 2005.
10. A Campaign for Real Milk, A Project of the Weston A. Price Foundation; www.realmilk.com
11. Ron Schmid, *The Untold Story of Milk*, New Trends Publishing, 2003, pp. 367–8.

12. A.J. Hosier, 'Open-Air Dairying', *Journal of the Farmers' Club*, Part 6, November 1927.
13. 'Portable dairy parlour for top New-Zealand-style herd', *Western Morning News*, 20 November 2013; www.westernmorningnews.co.uk/Portable-dairy-parlour-New-Zealand-style-herd/story-20102504-detail/story.html.
14. Nick Snelgar, 'Maplefield Milk C.I.C., A brief history'; email: nick.snelgar345@btinternet.com.

Chapter 9: Wild new farms

1. Nigel Boatman, et al., 'Impacts of Agricultural Change on Farmland Biodiversity in the UK', 2007, op. cit.
2. Richard Isenring, 'Pesticides reduce biodiversity', *Pesticide News*, 88, June 2010, PAN Europe.
3. European wild bird indicators 2008, European Bird Census Council (EBCC).
4. P.F. Donald, et al., 'The Common Agricultural Policy, EU enlargement and the conservation of European farmland birds', *Agriculture, Ecosystems and Environment*, 89(3), 2001, pp. 167–82.
5. *Agriculture in the UK*, Department for Environment, Food and Rural Affairs, 2015.
6. *Agriculture at a Crossroads*, 2008, op. cit.
7. David Thomas, 'A Study on the Mineral Depletion of the Foods Available to Us as a Nation Over the Period 1940 to 1991', *Nutrition and Health*, 2003, vol. 17, pp. 85–115.
8. Chloe Lambert, 'Best Before: Is the way we produce and process food making it less nourishing?', *New Scientist*, 17 October 2015, pp. 32–7.

9. John Reeves, 'The rise and fall of food minerals', *Nutrition and Health*, vol. 20, 2011, pp. 209–30.
10. D.A. Wardle, 'How plant communities influence decomposer communities', in R.D. Bardgett, M.B. Usher and D.W. Hopkins, eds, *Biological Diversity and Function in Soils*, Cambridge University Press, 2005, pp. 119–38.
11. Bethanie Afton, 1997, op. cit.
12. G.P.H. Chorley, 'The agricultural revolution in Northern Europe, 1750–1880: Nitrogen, legumes and crop productivity', *Agricultural History Review*, XXXIV, 1981, pp. 78, 92.
13. Bethanie Afton, 1997, op. cit., p. 5.
14. Royal Commission on Agriculture, 1895, [C.7624] XV19.
15. Frank Newman Turner, 1951, op. cit., pp. 67–8.
16. A. Luscher, et al., 'Potential of legume-based grassland-livestock systems in Europe: a review', *Grass and Forage Science*, Special issue: Forage legumes, vol. 69, issue 2, 2014, pp. 206–28. DOI: 10.1111/gfs.12124.
17. D.M. Broom, et al., 'Sustainable, efficient livestock production with high biodiversity and good welfare for animals', *Proceedings of the Royal Society B*; rspb.royalsocietypublishing.org/content/280/1771/20132025.

Chapter 10: Our grass-fed future

1. Allen R. Williams, 'Financial analysis shows grass-fed beef is good for producers', Organic Broadcaster/Moses Organic; www.mosesorganic.org/farming/farming-topics/livestock/grass-fed-beef-is-good-for-producers/.
2. www.jakofarm.com/skin-care/.

Index